Contents

'And what,' said Gobind on Sunday evening, 'is your honoured craft, and by what means earn you your daily bread?'

'I am,' said I, 'a kerani – one who writes pen upon paper, not in the service of the Government.'

'Then what do you write?' said Gobind...

'I write of all matters that lie within my understanding, and many that do not. But chiefly I write of Life and Death, and men and women, and Love and Fate according to the measure of my ability, telling the tale through one, two, or more people.'

Life's Handicap Rudyard Kipling *1891*

Best wishes to you, Joe,

from James

July 30 2019

WRITING FICTION
a user-friendly guide

JAMES ESSINGER

By the same author

*Jacquard's Web: how a hand loom led to
the birth of the information age*
(2004)

*Spellbound: the surprising origins and
astonishing secrets of English spelling*
(2007)

*Ada's Algorithm:
how Lord Byron's daughter Ada Lovelace
launched the digital age*
(2014)

The Mating Game
(2016)
(with Jovanka Houska)

Josh Moonford and the Lost City of Cantia
(2019)

*Frankie:
how one woman prevented a pharmaceutical disaster*
(2019)
(with Sandra Koutzenko)

This book is dedicated to
Russell Galen

Writing Fiction

Published by The Conrad Press in the United Kingdom 2019

Tel: +44(0)1227 472 874
www.theconradpress.com
info@theconradpress.com

ISBN 978-1-911546-54-2

Copyright © James Essinger 2019

The moral right of James Essinger to be identified as author of this work has been asserted in accordance with the Copyright, Designs and Patents Act 1988.

All rights reserved.

Typesetting and cover design by:
Charlotte Mouncey, www.bookstyle.co.uk

The Conrad Press logo was designed by Maria Priestley.

Printed and bound in Great Britain
by Clays Ltd, Elcograf S.p.A.

Preface

The purpose of this guide is to address a fascinating problem: how should one write fiction and are there any useful rules we can identify that will help any fiction writer to write more effectively?

This is designed to be a fairly informal guide. The suggestions in it derive from my own thinking and practice, and from my sessions coaching fiction writers in whose work my literary agency, Canterbury Literary Agency, has taken an interest.

Professionally, as well as running a literary agency, I write narrative non-fiction as well as fiction, and I also run a publishing firm, The Conrad Press. I am in fact probably better known for my narrative non-fiction than for my fiction, but while many of the rules for writing fiction apply to writing narrative non-fiction, fiction is harder to write - or at least harder to write well - mainly because by definition the story you're telling in a novel or short story is a fabrication, and so you don't start with the enormous advantage of a story that is true. No, when you write fiction you need to make your story *seem* true. If you succeed, your fiction may in fact seem truer than a non-fiction story.

I tend to think that for all human activity, there are a set of rules and that if you know what the rules are you can learn them, apply them, and be successful at the activity. You still need a certain amount of natural talent, but if you work hard and are willing to learn, you can improve your performance at writing fiction as at any other activity, and can indeed eventually perform at a level which may surprise you.

For example, playing chess, which is a game I enjoy, though I play it less often nowadays than I used to, is not as difficult as writing good fiction by any means, but there are certain practical strategic and tactical guidelines in chess which, by and large, you have to learn if you want to play well. This is also true of writing fiction.

A book you will probably find interesting is *How Not to Write a Novel* (Penguin Books 2009) by Sandra Newman and Howard Mittelmark. This is often very funny and full of lots of pithy advice about the pitfalls you should avoid when writing fiction. It is worth reading for its entertainment value alone.

The authors of *How Not to Write a Novel* are essentially saying, 'we can't really tell you very much about how to write fiction but we can tell you how *not* to do it'. The book is pretty useful all the same as it gives lots of examples of typical mistakes would-be fiction writers make, and if you can avoid all those mistakes you're probably well on your way to getting somewhere with your fiction-writing. I am going to be starting this guide by talking about some of the material in *How Not to Write a Novel*.

I do think, though, that the authors have to some extent evaded the question by producing a book called *How Not to Write a Novel*. They do list in detail many mistakes aspiring fiction writers make and clearly you can to some extent by a reverse extrapolation work out from the mistakes they list what you *should* be doing, but the authors provide no extensive answers to the question: *how should you write fiction?* Also, the book often reads as if it was written partly to mock unpublished fiction writers, whereas if those writers were given the right advice, maybe they wouldn't stay unpublished.

The whole business of how to write fiction interests me a great deal, partly because - unlike most human activities, e.g. running a business, or playing golf, tennis, or any other specialised activity - there is a shortage of good books about it. Indeed, if you think about it, there's a *bizarre* shortage of good books about how to write fiction.

I think there are three main reasons for this.

Firstly, the people whom you would ideally want to teach you how to write fiction would be successful published novelists, just as if you wanted to read a book that could teach you how to play better chess, you'd want to learn from an expert chess-player. But the reason why expert chess-players often write books about how to play chess well is because, except for those at the very top, playing chess is, unfortunately, not an especially well-paid job and if you're a chess grandmaster, earning a few thousand pounds from writing a chess book may be an important part of your income.

That's not true for successful writers. I'd love to read a book by, for example, Ken Follett about how to write fiction, and in fact on his website there is some very good guidance for fiction-writing - just as there is on the website of the United States science-fiction writer Robert Sawyer. This is generous of these writers; most successful fiction writers don't provide such information on their websites, or anywhere else, because they can earn far more from actually writing fiction than by writing about how to write it.

Two notable exceptions to the rule, though, that successful fiction writers don't write books about how to write fiction are Stephen King, whose book *On Writing* (2012) has been very well received, and David Lodge, whose *The Art of Fiction* (2011) is both a great read and an easy way to enjoy some illustrative passages by brilliant writers.

Secondly, people who are very good at practising some difficult profession are not always in fact the best teachers of that profession, so maybe many excellent writers of fiction might not *necessarily* be too good at teaching it.

Thirdly, I think many fiction writers don't want to encourage competition!

So yes, one of the problems of writing fiction is that there aren't many books about it and indeed there aren't many sources of information about writing good fiction at all. Because of this, it's horribly easy for would-be fiction writers to spend a huge amount of time that is mostly wasted, on writing fiction which doesn't actually work.

I think there is a need for a short, pithy book about how to write fiction successfully, a book that isn't too dogmatic but which proposes a number of rules which I think work in pretty much every case. I'm not suggesting *Writing Fiction - a user-friendly guide* is the only book you will need if you want to learn how to write fiction, but it should get you started.

Finally, my good friend the screenwriter and novelist William Osborne - whose many movie credits include co-writing the wonderful film *Twins* (1985) - read an earlier draft of this book and made many comments, some of which I'm including here attributed to him.

I have also been fortunate enough to have been given some advice by the legendary screenwriter Bob Gale, creator of the three *Back to the Future* movies. I am extremely grateful to Bob for his time and effort.

James Essinger   Canterbury, UK, April 2019

1. So what is fiction, anyway?

Let's start by thinking about what fiction is, and how it might have originated.

Fiction is really the modern equivalent of the tale told around the camp-fire in the distant past, when most people couldn't read or write, and indeed in the even more distant past (which for all practical purposes means longer than about 8,000 years ago) when written language hadn't even been invented.

People probably had quite mundane lives and would some evenings be visited by a tale-teller who would travel from one village to the other, and was paid by the village, and would move on after a while. He or she - though I suppose it was more likely a man in those days - would tell them stories that would entertain them after their daily toil in the fields.

I think this is a good starting-point for thinking about what fiction should be, because thinking about the tale-teller round the camp-fire makes us realise that people who have done a hard day's work don't really want to hear an everyday, uninteresting story about people like them. They want to hear a story which makes them feel that life is exciting, wonderful, and glorious.

And that's how the notion of the heroic story came about. It's a story about a person - it could be a man or a woman - who is not very bothered by everyday matters. That person was more concerned with doing heroic things, dealing with major problems, and he or she was someone who would inspire ordinary people because they wanted to be like that hero. Nor was that hero person very much like them.

Now that kind of hero is still a feature of much written fiction and many movies. By the way, I include movie stories in the discussions in this book, because after all, novels and movies are trying to do the same thing: they are both trying to tell a great story, and most of the story-telling tips that apply to novels also apply to movies, especially as of course many movies are based around novels anyway.

To take one or two examples of the kind of hero I mentioned just now, the characters Arnold Schwarzenegger plays in many of his movies aren't too bothered by the concerns of earning a living or worrying about whether they can pay the mortgage next month. Similarly, the character who Clint Eastwood plays in many of his movies is a person who is not usually very connected with everyday society. He's a sort of mythic traveller living outside the realm of everyday life. In films such as *The Outlaw Josey Wales* (1976) or *Pale Rider* (1985), Eastwood depicts a hero who moves from one community to the other and doesn't put down much in the way of ties once he's carried out his mission to expunge evil from the community.

To come more up to date, Lee Child's character Jack Reacher is really a pure heroic fantasy. Reacher is tall and very strong. He's a cop but he's very much a maverick; practically every woman he meets falls in love with him, he tends to hang around in late-night diners in New York, sipping coffee from a foam cup rather than a crockery one, as that way if he needs to move on quickly he can.

So I think the first and most fundamental thing we need to say about a work of fiction is that it needs to have a hero.

Or heroine. But I don't want to keep writing 'hero or heroine', so let's assume that 'hero' embraces 'heroine' (which might, incidentally, be a good way to end your story if it has a hero *and* a heroine.)

Now of course there are heroes and heroes. All that can usefully be said about heroes in the very sophisticated world of the dramatic narratives of today is that the hero has to be interesting, and entertaining to read about.

David Lodge's excellent novel *Nice Work* (1986) is set both in the academic world and industrial world of the British Midlands, in a city called Rummidge, based on Birmingham. Its hero is a rather short, slightly overweight, factory owner called Vic Wilcox and the book starts with Vic waking up in the morning, worrying about the factory he runs.

Vic Wilcox is not a hero in a conventional sense, but nevertheless he is one. During the story, even though he is already married, he beds the beautiful lady academic Robyn Penrose, the heroine, who has been sent to shadow him. He loses his job at the end of the book but he ends up with a new career as an entrepreneur. Certainly, Vic is a hero for our times in many respects and he stands up surprisingly well against more traditional heroes.

The anti-hero, someone who on the face of it is simply a villain, is also a kind of hero. An example of an anti-hero is the eponymous main character of the film *The Terminator* (1984) where it's quite clear that the cyborg played by Arnold Schwarzenegger really becomes in effect something of a hero of the piece, which has two other heroes: the woman the Terminator is trying to kill, and the soldier from the future who is trying to save her.

The Terminator does many amazing and extremely entertaining things. He can stop lorries, he can survive gunshot wounds, car crashes and he can even survive being incinerated. After a while we pretty much sympathise with him, because ultimately he's only a machine that's been programmed. It isn't as if he even has any personal animosity towards the woman he is trying to kill. In the sequel to the first Terminator movie, *Terminator 2: Judgement* Day (1991), another Terminator (also played by Arnold Schwarzenegger) is reprogrammed to be a good Terminator and is just as convincing being good as when he was evil.

So yes, to some extent we do sympathise with the evil Terminator just as we sympathise with the good one. And that's another point: a hero needs to be a character for whom we have some sympathy, or we won't care enough about the hero to be interested in him and what he is getting up to.

Frederick Forsyth's thriller *The Day of the Jackal* (1971)

offers another take on the hero, an extraordinary paradox of a hero who is not only an assassin and a murderer, but also who we know before the book starts does not succeed in his task because by the time the book was published, his target French president Charles de Gaulle was dead, and had died peacefully in his bed. (Forsyth points this out about midway through the book, presumably to avoid any accusations that he was hoping some readers wouldn't know that De Gaulle was not assassinated.)

When Forsyth tried to get his novel published it was turned down by several publishers. They didn't understand what he was trying to do. They thought 'why publish a book when we know from the start that the hero fails?' It was only when a publisher started to think, 'wait a minute, this is an interesting idea. The author is going to try to show us how close the assassin got to completing his job' that Forsyth received a publication offer for his book. At a technical level, Forsyth tells his story very well. *The Day of the Jackal* is a highly successful thriller and was deservedly a bestseller. It's not a great work of literature but it's stimulating, exciting and very entertaining.

We certainly are invited to sympathise with the Jackal. Forsyth invites us to approve of the Jackal's courage, his meticulous preparations, his technical competence, his passion to complete his mission, his seductive charm with women, and his love of the high life.

In a similar way, we find Hannibal Lecter in the stories by Thomas Harris a heroic character for several reasons, including that we are invited to think that the people he kills mostly deserve it, and that he likes politeness, has a sense of justice, is a bon viveur and connoisseur, and doesn't in fact kill people, such as Clarice Starling, if he finds the world 'more interesting' with them in it.

Generally, we must perhaps be careful not to be too dogmatic about what a hero should be like. Maybe indeed all we can really say is that a hero has to be engaging, interesting and someone with whom we can sympathise, at least to some extent. Oh, and of course the hero must be pretty much the main character in the story.

The hero needs to be at the centre of the piece. The hero could be a man or a woman, it could be an alien, it could be many things. The hero could be an animal, an invertebrate or even an inanimate object, like a chair or a table, it could be almost anything really, but at any rate the hero is an entity around whom the story focuses. In Roald Dahl's story *James and the Giant Peach* (1961) the secondary hero of the story is, as the title suggests, a giant peach.

Every good story, and ultimately a good novel is simply a long good story, has a hero.

A hero can even be a fairly normal person who becomes special and heroic because of what they're doing in the story. For example, Harold Fry in *The Unlikely Pilgrimage of Harold Fry* (2012) by Rachel Joyce, is a pretty ordinary bloke in most respects, but becomes heroic when he sets out to walk more than 600 miles, in yachting shoes, to help a friend.

So those are some thoughts about what a hero should be like.

Now let's look at a story in which a hero is actually operating. So, what makes a good story?

2. Devising a compelling story

The first, absolutely vital, thing to say - if you want your story to engage and entertain not only your aunt Mildred, or your sister Ethel, or your best friend, or your partner, but people who are strangers and who don't have any inherent interest in you i.e. the vast majority of the people you want as readers - is that *your story needs to have something significant at stake*. That is, your hero needs to be grappling with a problem that the reader (or audience) recognises as significant.

The nature of what is at stake will often depend to a large extent on the genre of the work in question. Literary novels often have things at stake that are actually very personal and emotional and not on the face of it especially big in the whole scheme of things; though if the story is sufficiently well told we will care about the issue all the same.

I must admit I personally tend to prefer stories that do have big things at stake. So for example, the movie *Armageddon* (1998) has the future survival of the world at stake, *Jurassic Park* (1993) the whole question of whether dinosaurs can be safely brought back to life, *Gladiator* (2000) whether Rome should be ruled by a murderous tyrant or by a wise and benevolent Senate.

In the novel *Gorky Park* (1981) and the fine movie based on it, *Gorky Park* (1983), what is at stake is whether the United States villain John Osborne (Jack Osborne in the movie) can break the Soviet monopoly on sables. I admire the book and the movie, but I always feel that 'the break the Soviet sable monopoly plot' was never very interesting. In fact, by the end of the book and movie, we are much more interested in the relationship between Arkady and Irina than in whether the Soviet monopoly on sables gets broken or not.

And that leads to an important subsidiary point: just having a big thing at stake will not make your story interesting if you don't tell it in an interesting way through bringing to life the struggles the characters face. Conversely, if a story is very good indeed, we may overlook the fact that nothing too significant is really at stake, which is arguably to some extent true with the *Gorky Park* book and movie. Will Osborne (no relation to John Osborne in *Gorky Park*) comments here *'I agree with you that the characterisation was brilliant and an excellent* mise en scene *but the "what if?" factor was poor. Ask yourself "what if Arkady failed, what would happen?"* This is, I think, a very reasonable comment: after all if the sables had made it to America and been released I can't imagine the world would have changed very much. I always felt that if sables could be reared successfully in the United States even during the Soviet times it's likely there would have been some sort of US/Soviet venture to make that happen, even during the Cold War.

Charles Dickens's novels tend to have very little at stake really except the redemption in some way of some of the leading characters in the story. Dickens himself once commented that all his novels are about redemption. However, the stories are generally good enough for us to feel that this is enough. This said, not all of his novels e.g. *Barnaby Rudge* (1841) are read much nowadays and many people know his work through movie or TV adaptations rather than because they've read the books. Moreover, *Our Mutual Friend* (1865), my personal favourite Dickens novel, is also not read much nowadays. I would argue that *A Christmas Carol* (1843) is an even better book, but at only 28,912 words long it is a novella or long short story rather than a novel.

Most nineteenth-century novels only had the personal fates of the hero or heroine and of some other characters at stake: the notion of the 'high-concept' story, where big things that go beyond the hero's personality are at stake, was very much a twentieth-century invention.

Overall, I recommend that you give very careful thought, before you start telling your story, to what is going to be at stake for your hero and/or heroine. Have something at stake that is inherently interesting and exciting, and you will begin the process of creating your story with a very significant headstart.

The writer Dan Harmon has set down a general formula for what makes a good story. I think on the whole it's a pretty good formula, and at the very least it's a great starting-point for any discussion about how a good story should be constructed.

There are eight stages in Harmon's formula, as follows. The italicised words are Dan's: the comments - in parentheses - mine:

1. *We start with the character* (Yes, we can call this character the hero).

2. *The character wants something* (I agree: there absolutely *must* be something at stake for the hero in the story, or the story can't be a story. You can't have a story about nothing).

3. *The character enters a new world* (Yes, but this doesn't need to be a world like in a fantasy novel; it can just be a new situation, such as a new job, a new relationship or a new house).

4. *The character adapts to the new world.*

5. *The character gets what they want.*

6. *The character suffers as a result.*

7. *The character returns to the ordinary world.* (Harmon regards this as the world the character came from, and which the character inhabited at the start of the story, by definition in an unsatisfactory way, because out of the unsatisfactoriness came the need which drove the progression of the story in the first place).

8. *The character changes as a result.*

Will: *'This is all you need - the 'monomyth' outlined by the Jungian anthropologist Joseph Campbell in his book, The Hero With The Thousand Faces (1949). He diagnosed the unifying narrative found in all human cultures through time: the hero with no parents who receives an unlikely calling, who embarks on a quest, befriends a buddy or buddies on his way, meets a wizened old man, is assigned tasks, before finally confronting and defeating the monster in his lair.'*

Consider how well that fits, for example, to the overall story of Harry Potter, and to many other great stories.

Many great stories, from fables about travelling into the underworld, and including most Shakespeare plays - *As You Like It* (1603) is a particularly useful example - and also most modern TV series and movies, can be successfully analysed using this formula and are often very good stories. There are sometimes variants on the formula, but the formula really does work.

For example, consider the first *Back to the Future* movie (1985) in the *Back to the Future* trilogy. I've chosen this movie here partly because it is such a good example of Dan's formula at work, and because it was made a sufficiently long time ago for you most likely to have seen it already and so I probably won't spoil it for you by making revelations of plot points. In fact, it's now some years beyond even 2015, the futuristic year to which Marty travels in the second *Back to the Future* movie.

At the start of the first movie, the hero Marty, who lives

in 1985, wants a new life, though he doesn't consciously articulate that need. The crass bully Biff is his father's work supervisor: his father has a lowly job as an office clerk. Marty accidentally and unintentionally travels back to 1955 in a time-machine built by his eccentric scientist friend Doc Brown in 1985. Marty adapts to this new time with the help of the 1955 counterpart of his friend Doc Brown.

Stuck in 1955, Marty has for the first time a pressing need he articulates: to get back to the future. After many struggles and physical challenges, Marty returns to 1985, where he finds that his entire family is different, as due to his father's new assertiveness that he, Marty, helped to prompt, his father is now richer, more successful and much more sorted than he was before, while Biff is now an abject and fawning weakling who runs a car servicing business.

Some viewers regard the story as having a logical flaw: Marty's mum and dad would, in fact, remember Marty from 1955, but that problem isn't explored, and it doesn't need to be.

(When I mentioned this possible 'logical flaw' to Bob Gale, he replied as follows, which seems to me a more than adequate reply; he also mentions a *real* logical flaw which he does concede exists. I don't believe, however, that the real logical flaw will dent anyone's love of the *Back to the Future* movies, and in fact until Bob mentioned it to me this particular matter hadn't occurred to me at all. As Bob says: *Yes, many people have asked why George and*

Lorraine don't remember Marty. Well, they do remember him, but only as a kid who showed up at their high school for a few days thirty years ago. Think back on people you knew very briefly when you were a teenager. How well would you remember them? Without a photo, could you clearly remember their faces? I have looked at my high school yearbook many times, and there are an incredible number of people I don't recall even when I see their picture! And so, I believe it would never, ever occur to you that your own child, whom you saw every day from the day he was born, could possibly be that same person who drifted through your school. The real logical flaw goes past almost everyone -- it relates to the "disappearing photo." Why are only the images disappearing instead of the physical photo itself? And who would have taken the photo, especially by the end, when Marty is being erased from existence? But it's another example of a plot device with rules that we live by, and then it returns as an important plot device in Part 3.)

Of all of Dan's rules, there can be no doubt that it is the hero's *need* that matters most. This goes back to the piece of advice with which I started this chapter. What is at stake for your hero? What does your hero pressingly need how does that need change as the story progresses? In fact every good story is about a hero's *quest* to achieve something. When you're planning your novel's story, think what quest your hero could be on, and that will very likely lead you to decide what is at stake for your hero and what your novel should be about.

While it is indeed a legitimate criticism of *How not to Write a Novel* that it is better at pointing out what not to do than what to do, there is a useful passage on the very first page of Part 1, which *does* offer great advice about how to devise a great story. Here it is:

Typically the plot of a good novel begins by introducing a sympathetic character who wrestles with a thorny problem. As the plot thickens, the character strains every resource to solve the problem, while shocking development and startling new information help or hinder her on the way. Painful inner conflicts drive her onward but sometimes also paralyse her at a moment of truth. She finally overcomes the problem in a way that takes the reader totally by surprise, but in retrospect seems both elegant and inevitable.

Here, for 'she' also read 'he', of course. Hero or heroine, heroine or hero, ultimately the story of any great novel charts the progress of the lead character's quest towards their true destiny.

3. Two golden rules:
1) stick to your story;
2) make your hero an active participant in it

Here are two golden rules which most would-be fiction writers ignore and then are surprised when their book gets rejected.

Firstly, in order for your story to have a chance of being interesting, by and large it needs to be pretty economical, which means you have to stick to the story and not deviate too much from it.

This is where many first-time fiction writers come unstuck. They put in too much unnecessary detail, and it strangles their story. *In a professional-quality novel, every detail needs to advance the core story somehow*. So, stick to your story.

Yes, every detail must count. If the detail doesn't advance the story, delete it.

Secondly, your hero must be an *active participant in* the story. This may sound obvious, but many writers who set out to try to write fiction have too much *being done* to the hero, rather than the hero actually *doing things. The Day of the Jackal* has things being done to the hero; the police are, after all, trying to catch him, but he never stops being resourceful himself, and never stops initiating things.

While I admire J. K. Rowling's achievement very much, one of the problems I have with the *Harry Potter* stories is that Harry is often - though not always - a fairly passive hero. At crucial dramatic points in the stories, especially when he is facing apparent great peril, he gets rescued by a *deus ex machina.* This is a Latin expression that means 'the god from the scaffolding' and refers to the technique of solving the problems in a Classical play by a god coming down and sorting everything out. Nowadays the expression is used to refer to a contrived solution to a character's difficulties that dissatisfies us because the contrivance is so blatant and doesn't seem to harmonise with the preceding story. I think this is a fair criticism, for example, of the scene in the *Harry Potter and the Prisoner of Azkaban* movie (2004) when Harry is rescued from apparently certain death at the claws of the werewolf by the hippogriff.

The trouble with writers using this technique, especially when they use it in a series of books about the same character, is that pretty soon we cease to believe that the character is ever likely to be in any real danger *at all.* Harry Potter himself is active enough in the stories for the stories to work - for example, in the same Prisoner of Azkaban movie, there is a wonderful scene where Harry uses the Patronus spell to defeat the Dementors - but I would say that the stories work more because of the wonderful imagination the author pours into them, and because of all the other characters, than because Harry is enormously interesting himself. Fortunately, Hermione definitely is.

We are likely to be less interested in a hero who is passive and to whom things are purely done to. I know there are some erotic novels where that is so! But that's rather a special case. In most novels we need a hero who is very active. This is why detective novels or novels about people who fight crime are often successful, because they have a ready-made hero - the detective - and also they have a ready-made scenario where the hero is investigating a murder. It's an inherently dramatic and engaging story-line.

4. Lessons from Hollywood

As you might expect, there are indeed many correlations between writing dramatic narrative fiction in novels and writing screenplays. Pretty much every rule that applies to making a good story in a novel also applies to what makes a good story in a movie.

There are many pieces of advice about writing movie stories that work when writing fiction: we've already seen some when looking at devising a story. Here are two more that I find very useful:

1. *Get into the scene as late as you can, and get out of it as soon as you can.* That's excellent advice. Only give the crucial dramatic elements of the scene.

2. *Under no circumstances make your hero's task easy.* After all, if you were writing a crime thriller and on the very first page the detective found some information that let him or her know who the killer is, there wouldn't actually be a story. Of course, no writer would be so foolish as to make a story that's one page long; all the same, many screenplays - both made and unmade - do make the hero's job too easy. That's lazy writing. Stories where that's not the case are more engaging and more interesting, essentially

because we get a vicarious thrill from experiencing
the ebb and flow of the character's fortunes,
which we also feel mirrors the ups and downs of
life generally.

One of many reasons why the *Back to the Future* trilogy is
so successful is because in each film the characters confront
a specific problem which is extremely hard to solve. I've
already mentioned the challenge Marty faces in the first
movie of getting back to 1985. Specifically, in the first film
Marty and Doc Brown have to find a way of getting enough
energy into the car to send Marty back to the time where
he belongs. The only way they can think of doing this is
to channel a bolt of lightning into the car.

In the second film they have to reverse an unfortunate
change to the space-time continuum inadvertently caused
by Marty and in the third film they have a simpler task
- although it's still very difficult in 1885 - of getting their
car up to 88 mph, the speed it has to go to become a time
machine. I'd often wondered whether when - in the first
movie - 88 mph was chosen as the speed the car would
need to attain, the writer already planned that the third
film would be set in the Wild West, where reaching 88
mph was an extremely difficult task. If the speed had
been lower, there might not have been such a challenge
and the entire plot of the third film would have had to
be rethought.

Will Osborne suggested I try to find out what the real
situation was as regards the writing of *Back to the Future*.

So, nothing daunted, I contacted the Hollywood agency that represents the screenwriter Bob Gale and sent him an email regarding this very matter. To my delight Bob replied within twenty-four hours saying the following. The parentheses are Bob's.

When we made the first movie, we were not thinking about a sequel, much less two. It was just going to be a 'one-off' film. We selected 88 miles per hour as the speed of the car because we thought it would be easy for people to remember, and it was faster than anyone would 'accidentally' drive a car. (Trivia note - the stock DeLorean speedometer only went up to 85, a fact unknown to us until we got our hands on a car, so the speedometer shots in the movie are of a different car.) With all of our time travel rules set up in the first movie, we had to adhere to those in the sequels -- absolutely required in writing: establish rules and live by them. We thought it fitting that since the time travel problem in the first movie was about power, in the 3rd it should (and could) be about speed. For further info about the writing of the movies, you should watch the documentaries that are included in the recent video releases, either the 25th or 30th Anniversary sets and/or the 2015 book 'Back to the Future: The Ultimate Visual History.'

I felt I had to email Bob to ask whether he therefore saw it as serendipity to have chosen the speed of 88 mph for the first film. Bob emailed me back to say:

I don't think there's a person on this Earth who doesn't look back at Good Fortune and say, thank goodness I did it this way instead of that way. And of course, the opposite is also true when we have bad fortune, over which we are perpetually asking ourselves, oh why did I do it that way?

But writing is also to a great extent problem-solving. In this specific instance, we needed to create a challenge for ourselves in the third movie, and if it hadn't been about the speed of the vehicle, we would have come up with something else. That said, given that the speed of the vehicle had already been set in stone at 88 miles per hour, we never once thought about how fortuitous that choice had been. So by the time we did part three, the 88 miles per hour aspect was to us as natural as the fact that a man has two legs. We never ruminated about either one of those concepts!

A big thank-you to Bob Gale for taking the trouble to answer my questions in such detail.

The *Back to the Future* stories ingeniously make the characters' challenges about as difficult as we can imagine them being. Pretty much every possible opportunity for making the challenges difficult is brought into the service of the screenplay. For example, in the first film, just before the lightning bolt is to be channelled into the car, Doc Brown is using a rather complicated system of wires to try to do this and the hands on the town hall clock as pivots. One of the wires comes off the clock hand and it's only absolutely in the nick of time that Doc Brown is able to re-attach the wires so the lightning bolt can discharge into the car Marty's in.

So yes, you need to make your hero or heroine's job

difficult, sometimes so difficult that the readers or audience wonder how anyone could pull it off.

Yet the same readers or audience *don't mind* a hero or heroes having a certain amount of luck. Almost standard in any movie and in any thriller is that the hero faces apparently insurmountable odds but has certain strokes of luck which we're happy to believe, if we feel they're plausible.

For example, in the second *Lord of the Rings* movie, *The Two Towers* (2002), there's a scene where a few hundred warriors in Helms Deep are about to be attacked by an army of about ten thousand orcs. And it seems the defenders have absolutely no way of surviving this. However, at the last minute a contingent of elves arrives, maybe a thousand, and then a little later the Riders of Rohan arrive under Gandalf's leadership, and soon a forest of the lugubrious tree-characters, the Ents, decide they're going to help, and they become allies with the people of Helms Deep as well. Later, during the battles, there's a flood that washes many of the orcs away, and the remnant run into the forest where they are killed by the ents. It feels satisfying. We don't feel cheated. Yes, we don't mind a hero having some luck. After all, that mirrors life; you do need a certain amount of luck if you want to get on.

Another lesson from Hollywood is this: if you can't put a summary of your story on the back of a postcard then your story is too complicated. Hollywood would probably say nowadays - as we don't use postcards much anymore - that if you can't furnish a summary of your story which could be told to a studio executive during a ride in an elevator you've probably got a story that's either not sufficiently focused, or too complicated. Hence the origin of the term 'elevator pitch'.

All the best stories can be summarised quite briefly. Essentially, your novel should in effect be a powerful, dramatic and compelling elaboration of the summary of your story.

5. The importance of a good outline

Most inexperienced fiction writers (and some experienced, published ones) waste time when they set out to write a novel because they don't bother to work out in advance what their story is before they start writing it.

They often fall too much in love with the writing process and are more interested in doing the writing than in deciding what their story really is.

I have often made this mistake myself in the past. All I can say is, adopting that lackadaisical attitude towards writing your novel is likely to involve you in much wasted time, and may indeed so sap your energies that your novel never gets finished at all, or if you do finish it, your book may not be much good.

It's much better to work out in advance the story you want to tell, and what will be at stake for your hero or heroine. But do leave some opportunities for flexibility in the plan: you'll want to have things to discover as you write the book, and you'll want to give yourself the opportunity to include new plot developments that you think will work.

In the novel *The Mating Game* (2016) for example, authored by myself and Jovanka Houska, we gave our heroine Vanny a passionate gay affair about half-way through the book because we felt strongly that we needed to take her out of her comfort zone. Her gay lover Helene became an important character in the story and readers generally took to her. We hadn't planned the character Helene when we were planning the story.

What, in summary, does the reader want in terms of a novel? I would say the reader wants something that is compelling, emotionally satisfying, doesn't have irrelevant digressions and has lots of ebbs and flows of fortune, and a dramatic climax.

You need to care about your readers and give them a great time. Be professional. Think of your readers as your customers, because that is exactly what they are.

I wonder whether we can draw an analogy here about falling in love with writing and falling in love with another person. When we are falling in love with another person, we very quickly learn that if we want *them* to like *us*, we have to pay attention to their agenda. If, for example, the other person has a job where they must go to bed at eleven o'clock at night, and they say to us, 'Look please don't phone me after ten o'clock because when we have our loving calls late at night I don't really sleep very well and it spoils my day the next day,' we've got a choice, either we're going to go along with that and keep them happy, or not.

If we then phone at half past ten and he or she says, 'I thought I asked you not to phone at half past ten?' and if we reply, 'Yes, I know you said that to me but actually, my feelings for you are so strong that I *want* to phone you at half past ten,' they would be justified in thinking we didn't deserve to have a relationship with them, even though they might actually like us.

Similarly, if we're going to be professional writers, we have to care about the reader's agenda. No ifs, no buts. If we're just going to want to spend our weekends and evenings writing some very lengthy, digressive novel which alludes to our childhood, our sex life (real or imagined), people we want to get revenge on, etc. etc, fine. I'm not saying don't use your time to do that if you want to, but don't expect to get the result published.

Your novel is not a diary of your life, nor an autobiography (though it may use autobiographical elements), it's a story designed to entertain and engage other people, most of whom will be strangers to you. The vast majority of your readers don't know you and don't inherently care about you, though if you tell them a great story that thrills them and entertain them, they might end up loving you, even if they're most likely never going to meet you. Maybe they would care about you if you met them at a dinner party, but they're unlikely to meet you at a dinner party. They don't know you.

If a novelist is only being read by people who really like him personally, he's not going to get much of a readership. There's an instructive line in T.S. Eliot's play *The Cocktail Party* (1949) where a male character is talking about the poetry of a female character, Celia. He says: 'Yes, I've seen her poetry - Interesting if one is interested in Celia.' And that really says it all about amateurish writing.

This is why publishers and agents are so wary, not just wary but irritated, if they are offered a novel along with a letter or email which says something like this, 'my friends/ mother/father/girlfriend really like it.' The publishers don't care what those people think, and justifiably not because after all those people are not actually going to pay to publish the novel. The publisher suspects that their standards are lower than his/her own standards will be, and that's indeed likely to be so. It might very rarely be the case that the author's friends and relatives are right, but then the book will most likely be so good that practically any publishing firm should at least consider publishing it. Alas, though, in the current abysmal publishing climate even great books by first-time novelists don't necessarily attract a deal, which is why I founded The Conrad Press, which uses a different business model to conventional publishing. Would *Harry Potter and the Philosopher's Stone* (1997) attract a deal nowadays if J.K. Rowling were an unknown writer starting out? Very possibly not. The book received many rejections even at the time, and the 1990s, when it was submitted, were a much more auspicious time for new writers than today.

In fact, when J.K. Rowling started her new writing career as a writer of adult thrillers, she submitted samples of her new novel, *The Cuckoo's Calling*, (2013) which she wrote under the pseudonym Robert Galbraith. They were all rejected with condescending rejection letters, at least one of which advised Mr Galbraith to go on a creative writing course! If you want to see some of these extraordinary but predictable letters, they are readily found on the internet if you search for 'J.K. Rowling rejection emails'.

Today, mainstream publishers are reluctant to publish novels by unknown writers at all; barely one percent of unknown writers' novels submitted by literary agents are accepted by mainstream publishers, and as that percentage is commercially not viable for an agent seeking to make a living, I tend to focus on representing non-fiction nowadays, though if I get a novel in which I absolutely adore, I will still try it on fiction editors, though not necessarily with much optimism. Otherwise I will steer a novel I like towards The Conrad Press.

Will Osborne suggested here: *'Perhaps add a postcript - explaining how fiction is now a fashion/marketing business the writer must not only write a good story but be as marketable as possible and create a "brand".'*

Yes, I totally agree. writers need to be seen as a brand if they are to be truely successful.

Going back to the main theme here, it's what people who *don't* know you think of your work that matters. Certainly, no-one who doesn't know you is likely to start with a preconceived dispensation to like your work, and that is essentially why the world of writing fiction can be a very tough world to break into, and indeed in which to make a living. But think of a story with a hero or heroine facing a perilous problem, and use your imagination to amplify your story *within* that remit, and stick to your story, and you might end up finding yourself surprised at your success.

Ultimately, any good story, as I've already indicated, is about the *quests* of the hero and the other main characters. Most good stories - indeed, maybe all good stories - are to some extent, indeed often to a large extent, at a very fundamental level, a quest.

What kind of quest? Well, that depends on the story you are telling. But here are some examples:

- a quest for love

- a quest to help someone

- a quest to save someone from something, including of course from death

- a quest to solve a perplexing mystery (in a crime story, the mystery often concerns who committed a crime)

- a quest to understand life better

- a quest for happiness

- a quest for understanding

- a quest to make something wonderful happen

- a quest to stop something terrible happening

- a quest to save and protect something the characters love and cherish.

Will Osborne adds here: *'and if you can put four or five of these types of quest in the same story so much the better!'* These are just some examples of quests we read about. The great thing about having a quest as your story is that even if your novel has some boring parts, and all novels have parts that some readers will find less interesting than other parts, the momentum of the reader's interest in the quest will keep the reader interested and wanting to read on. This is why Dickens's novels, which all have boring parts that tend to get cut in the movie or TV versions, stay readable and interesting overall: we find the characters' quests interesting.

Of course, as Will intimates, some stories have several quests in them; indeed some may contain all the above quests. But you need at least one major quest in your novel, and if you only do have one quest in it I recommend you make it a dramatically extremely important one.

There are, after all, great quests in life, too. For example, the greatest quest in the twentieth century was the quest to destroy Nazism and thereby to give the world the opportunity to move into what Winston Churchill called in his famous, thirty-six-minute inspirational speech in the House of Commons on the afternoon of June 18 1940, 'broad, sunlit uplands'. Fortunately for the world and humanity, that quest, which did indeed cost so much 'blood, sweat and toil', was successful.

6. Which writers should be your model?

It's all very well finding setting out to discover your own original voice as a novelist, but most writers find it easy to use some other writer as their model, especially at the start of their career. So which writers should you use as an inspiration, or as a model?

A big problem many writers have is that they take the wrong authors as models for their work. For example, when I began trying to write fiction back in the late-1970s, I tend to think I used Charles Dickens as my model. Very likely I did so unconsciously.

I studied Dickens at university. I've not read all his novels and I probably won't read them all now, but the novels of his that I have read I know very well, and I think I can say I know Dickens pretty well as a writer.

But using Dickens as a model was a mistake, and delayed my development as a fiction writer for several years.

As we're writing novels for the modern world, it makes more sense to take as your model modern writers who are successful today. Novels like *The Day of the Jackal, Nice Work* and Ken Follett's *Eye of the Needle* (1981), for example. I would regard *Nice Work* as a better novel than the other two, but that's just a matter of taste, really, and all the same *Eye of the Needle* and *The Day of the Jackal* were very successful. They are both excellent thrillers, not that subtle overall but they have many subtle moments. They're good examples, I think, of models to use if you want to be writing fiction today.

So, no, I don't recommend you use Dickens as your model or indeed any writer who was born much before 1930.

After all, Dickens was born in 1812 and died in 1870. He was writing during a strange time, pretty much technology-less by our standards, and about as different from our times as it is possible to imagine. The nineteenth century was full of long, dark evenings, when people had to amuse themselves by the light of candles or oil lamps. All of Dickens's novels - not some of them, all of them - were serialised, (though not his novellas/long short stories such as *A Christmas Carol*) - and it's a simple fact that even Dickens himself forgot some aspects of what was going on in his plots between the long process of writing the novels and issuing them in serial form. His longer novels amazingly actually took about two years to be fully issued in serials. These longer novels are about 375,000 words long.

You can't possibly, over two years, writing a serial every month or every week, create a taut, concise thriller. Of course we call *The Day of the Jackal* a novel, and we call *David Copperfield* (1850) a novel, but they're very different art forms.

It's interesting that later in his career Dickens became influenced by Wilkie Collins and began to write tauter novels which were much more like modern thrillers. *Our Mutual Friend*, the last novel Dickens completed, is quite a long novel, yet it has a much less rambling structure than his earlier novels and contains thriller elements. Of course Dickens was a great writer, and his reputation is justifiably immortal. But please don't use Dickens as your model. If Dickens wrote *David Copperfield* today I very much doubt that it would get published without a lot of editing.

Dickens's novels are often very poorly crafted by modern standards. Many of the characters don't come off. Many of the events in the stories are completely tangential to the action. TV and film adaptations of Dickens's novels tend to be crisp and focused, but the novels are often highly digressive.

For example, on the very first page of *David Copperfield* there's an extraordinary, absurd, almost 500-word digression, about David being born with something called a 'caul'. This is a harmless membrane inside which babies are sometimes born. For some reason, a dried caul was often bought by sailors in the past because they believed it would prevent them from being drowned. This seems to have derived from an old superstition - the origin is not clear - that a caul brought good luck. The 500 or so words that Dickens writes about the caul are completely irrelevant to the rest of the story. It's not as if the caul reappears anywhere else: it doesn't. Put in those kind of digressions nowadays and your editor (if you get as far as having an editor) is going to ask you why mention the caul at all. You can't do that today.

Joseph Conrad, another great writer, is possibly an even worse model for an aspiring writer. I'm in good company in thinking this: Graham Greene thought the same. I admire Conrad greatly, and indeed my decision to come and live in Canterbury back in 1986 was partly influenced by the fact that Conrad spent the last few years of his life near Canterbury and is buried here. Yes, Conrad is a great writer.

But he has many serious weaknesses. The worst one is that his female characters tend to be poorly drawn. His novels are also almost completely devoid of anything in the way of deep romantic feeling, and sexual feeling is in fact even more absent from Conrad's work than from Dickens's. Incidentally, I would agree with George Orwell in his excellent long essay on Dickens - first published in *Inside the Whale and Other Essays* (1940) - that Dickens's novels are less sexless than they are often regarded as being.

Conrad's novels are often morbid and even rather depressing, but the best ones are masterpieces all the same, mainly due to his almost superhuman ability to conjure mood and setting with words. They are masterpieces but they are not good models for being a writer. Like many writers, I went through a period of being influenced by Conrad: he has a particular appeal I think, for lonely, sex-starved young men, which I was in those days. He is probably an even worse model than Dickens. Graham Greene recounts in his autobiography *A Sort of Life* (1971) going through a phase of having Conrad as his model. Greene describes Conrad as a 'dangerous' model. Certainly, I think that if you try to imitate Conrad, you risk producing little except a pastiche of his strange and rather roundabout style, just as I once did.

So don't use inappropriate models, otherwise you may never get your literary career started at all. Modern popular novelists really are a more reliable model for you. I don't think you need to worry about the danger of emulating them too closely; after all, if we don't have our own ideas for our story and characterisations and our own conception of what our own novel should be, we're never going to be novelists anyway.

7. How long should your novel be?

Moving on now, what *length* should your novel be?
You have to be very, very talented to get a first novel published that's much longer than about 90,000 words. For subsequent novels it is different. Ideally your first novel shouldn't be much more than 75,000 words long. You are unlikely to get away with writing a novel the length of a Dickens novel unless you are writing in the fantasy genre, where great length is more acceptable, but don't imagine that editors of fantasy novels won't expect every word of your 250,000-word tome to count and have an impact, because they will. Indeed, unless you're incredibly talented or incredibly lucky you are unlikely to get away with a vast novel, and, even if you're both of those things your readers may, in fact, prefer a shorter one.

To return to a theme I have already touched on, the current time (I am writing this in March 2019) is an absolutely dreadful time for new writers, both in the UK and the US and - while those are the two markets I know about - no doubt in much of the rest of the world too. It's not a great time for even reasonably well-established writers, either. Advances have gone through the basement, and indeed many publishers have pretty much stopped publishing novels by first-time writers, though they rarely admit this, so unfortunate literary agents, and writers too, keep on sending publishers novels that are usually rejected.

But you can't really blame publishers for being wary of publishing a first novel even if it is very good: the simple fact is that first novels are hard to get published and noticed, so publishers are very wary of risking money on them. After all, if you were a publisher dependent on your profits for feeding your family, and you were offered a novel called, for example, *The Summer of Love of Cressida Taylor* by a well-known lady television personality, or the same book by a totally unknown lady writer, whose book would you publish... once you'd thought up a new title, anyway? Yes, exactly.

If someone writes, say, a new biography of Dickens, that is a newsworthy event (well, if it's a good biography anyway) but it's hard to dream up a newsworthy event about a novel by a new writer except relating to the size of the advance; indeed, for many overhyped novels by new writers, the size of the advance *is* the only really interesting thing about the book.

In the present climate, many publishers on both sides of the Atlantic won't even *read* a novel longer than 100,000 words. Bear that in mind if you want to get published.

True, sometimes a very long novel (and I regard any novel of more than 100,000 words in length as very long) can be successfully divided into two separate novels, which together in effect form a duology. But by and large I tend to think that any first-time writer who writes a novel longer than about 100,000 words probably has a secret subconscious desire not to get published.

8. The need to pursue everything

Another vital point: everything in your novel must be *pursued.*

What do I mean by pursued? It means this: all the details to which you draw the reader's attention must be revealed as an essential part of the story or you shouldn't include those details at all.

A novel is not real life. Real life is full of events that are fundamentally meaningless and often random. Many things we need to do to keep our bodies alive are essential for us, but are not invested with mythic and/or spiritual significance, which is why bestselling novels don't generally contain scenes of characters going to the lavatory after breakfast - well, with the exception of James Joyce's *Ulysses* (1922), anyway. But novels are a form of concentrated life that aspire to invest life with mythic and spiritual significance.

So all the things in your novel that seem slightly out of the ordinary - a character originating from Cornwall if your novel is set in England, or a character with (say) an artificial hand, or a non-Finnish character who spent time in Finland, to take just a few examples - need to be part of the plot somehow. If they aren't, why put those details in at all?

In real life unusual details usually don't get pursued. We just see things and take them for granted, and we just hear things and hear about things and we take them for granted, too. If you go to a dinner-party and meet a Moroccan guy there who is an expert at Moroccan cookery and who also has a Moroccan cobra, you just accept these facts as things that happen in life. But a novel is a story that needs to seem real and believable and has a power and energy and coherence about it that helps us to understand life and makes our lives more enjoyable. So if the Moroccan guy appears in a novel you quite rightly expect him to be an important element of the story, and maybe the cobra should play an important part in it, too. After all, if you have the Moroccan character in your novel and you never make any more of that, the reader might think: why is the character from Morocco, anyway? Why not from Manchester? Your character from Morocco should, in effect, justify where he comes by his 'Morocco-ness' being a vital part of the story. His being from Morocco needs to be followed up somehow. So, as I say, if you don't want to follow it up, don't put it in.

I suggested at the start of this book that novels most likely derived from camp-fire tales told ages ago. In any camp-fire tale, a tale-teller who came along and spent the first half hour talking about his walk to the field that morning and doing his usual daily work is probably not going to get very far as a tale-teller, as the village people would probably boot him out of the village. But it's not only that people listening to the tale-teller around the campfire don't want to hear about mundane things. They also don't want to be expected to focus on elements in the story that don't turn out to have any significance in it.

If, for example, one evening when everyone was gathered around the fire happily roasting their sausages on long forks and looking forward to be entertained, and the campfire tale-teller began his story by saying, 'I was setting out for the field last week and I happened to see an enormous turnip in the field I was working in, the biggest turnip I've ever seen,' and if the tale-teller never again mentioned that turnip you might think, why did he mention it in the first place? No campfire roast sausages for him.

Or imagine that, at the same dinner party, you start telling a story about your holiday in Spain last year, and you talk about a beautiful day you had in Toledo, and you recall that while driving to Toledo you saw a yellow Volkswagen overturned on the road; there had been a crash. Well, if you're telling that at a dinner party it's probably okay, because it's an anecdote about life, but if you're writing a novel we want and need to know about the yellow Volkswagen and if in fact there's no point to it in relation to the story, then don't put it into the story at all, just like the Moroccan guy and his cobra. The point is that the sentence you're telling at that particular moment becomes the crucial focus for the reader. *Also, and this is an absolutely vital point, the reader has no way of knowing that what you're telling him or her about at the moment is irrelevant to the rest of the story.* The reader needs to feel able to trust you. So if you're talking about a yellow Volkswagen we want to know more about it and why it's in the story. And if you don't seem to be making it a real part of the story the reader will wonder why you put it in at all, and will trust you less.

The rule is this: the details you're bringing to the attention of the reader must be made significant in the story. At one level, this is just basic common sense. It's also an artistic courtesy to the reader.

Moreover, the more interesting the detail, the more the reader is likely to expect it to be pursued.

For example, imagine if you're writing a love story about a humdrum relationship a man has with an unremarkable woman, let's call her Maud, and what happens is that the relationship gets better very slowly, the hero and Maud become close and eventually get married. In fact, I don't really advise you to write that story as it doesn't sound as if it would be a particularly interesting one.

But leaving that aside, let's have the hero (who, let's say, loves the poems of T.S. Eliot) travelling on the bus to the estate where Maud lives. It's a wet day. The bus stops for a moment at the bottom of a hill. Hurrying past the bus on the way to the railway station is another woman, the loveliest woman the hero's ever seen in his entire life. She's beautifully dressed, she doesn't look upset by the rain, she looks thoughtful, she looks interesting, especially as she's carrying under her arm a book he can see, even in the rain: a book of T.S. Eliot's poems.

Well, are your readers going to prefer to want him to

forget about this new woman and go to see Maud? No, because they'd want to know more about that particular woman because she's interesting and also because we feel that the hero could have a great life with her. I'm not saying a novel always has to be about positive things, but we want to feel excited and inspired by novels. Certainly, if I was reading an author's novel or the plan for the novel and I found the episode about his boring imminent life with Maud and his glimpse of the beautiful girl on the bus I'd say something like this to the author: 'abandon that Maud storyline, my friend. Let's have another storyline where the bus goes off up the hill, the hero sits there and thinks about the woman and he rings the bell, and the bus stops at the next stop, or even better he persuades the driver to stop the bus right away, and he runs down the hill, he finds the woman, and she's reached the railway station, she's about to get on the train and he turns and says to her, and says, "I love T.S. Eliot." She says, "Oh really? I've never met anybody else who loves T.S. Eliot in my entire life."' And they talk and she ends up getting a later train instead. Now you've got a story, or at least a beginning of one. That story's already got a bit of a life of its own, because at that point you're interested in the characters and care about them.

9. Character in your novel

Fiction is, above all a character-based art form. To make a story exciting and interesting you need to make it about people you care about. If you care about them yourself, and you've written your novel well enough it's a fair bet that your readers might find themselves caring about your characters too.

Make your characters complex and human and vulnerable and your readers will not only like them but may become so absorbed in their adventures they won't want to put the book down. Actually, it's easy to produce a novel your readers can't put down - you simply coat its covers in superglue - but a technique your readers will appreciate more is to give them a flawed, human, complicated but yet somehow admirable character and involve that character in a fast-paced, focused, irrelevancy-free and absorbing story. Oh, and for goodness' sake give your characters imperfections and flaws: just because you (probably) imagine yourself to be perfect in every way doesn't mean your characters need to be.

Ken Follett's novel *Eye of the Needle* is about a German spy who is trying to relay a crucial wartime secret to the Nazis. When his radio breaks, he tries to swim out to the Nazi submarine that has been sent to pick him up. Yet while the spy - codenamed 'The Needle' (you'll see now that the book's title is so brilliant) is certainly prepared to kill to achieve his ends - even kill people on his own side, he has many human vulnerabilities, and these make him likeable. He vomits after killing people, for example, he yearns for German sausages (not at the same time), he remembers his love affairs, in fact he's quite a many-sided character. We read on because we want to know what happens to the guy.

How do you create characters whom your readers will care about? Well, I'd say create characters you yourself find interesting and put them in tough, difficult but believable situations. I'm not sure how you can guess what kind of characters your readers will find interesting, and even if you could guess, then the characters still wouldn't be interesting if you didn't make them interesting yourself, so you do need to create characters you personally find interesting, and whom you strongly believe in.

Try to think of your characters as real people rather than characters in a novel. Will Osborne quotes Scott Fitzgerald's remark: 'Start out with a character and you end up with a stereotype, start out with a stereotype and you end up with nothing.'

What I think that means is that the process of writing is not kind to characters who have not been engineered as real people by the author. Start by thinking of your characters as real and there is a fair chance you will manage to embody that reality in the novel. On no account think of them as characters or stereotypes.

A crucial tip is to imagine your characters existing outside the confines of your novel. You should know more about them than actually appears in the novel. You should know what they would do in circumstances that may not even be depicted in the novel. Also, you should spend time with your characters imaginatively, just as you might spend time with your friends in reality. The more you know about your characters in your novel and the more you think about them, the more likely it is that they will come across as real people when the reader reads it.

10. Your novel's voice

Let's now move on to talking about the voice of your novel.

The question of the novel's voice is one of the big decisions you have to make before you start writing. By the voice of the novel I mean the answer to this crucial question: who is telling the story?

This is where there's a huge difference between the cinema and the novel. When you're writing a screenplay some things are fairly easy. The viewpoint is simply the dispassionate, disinterested camera. By the way, 'disinterested' means 'impartial' not 'uninterested', which means having no feelings of interest for something. These nuances of meaning are things you need to know about, or teach yourself about, if you want to be a published novelist.

You can still use someone's point of view quite effectively on the screen, though. For example, consider a particular scene in the movie *Planes, Trains and Automobiles* (1987) with Steve Martin and John Candy. It's about two men who are thrown together, a middle-class executive (Martin) and a working-class salesman (Candy) on a comically disastrous journey. At one point they arrive at a motel. There's only one room left in it so they have to share the room and they assume there will be two beds in it. When they get to the motel they find there's only one double bed and the movie's director, John Hughes, is very careful to show us Steve Martin's astonished face, then we see the camera panning over the double bed, so we see clearly Steve Martin's viewpoint. He's particularly horrified because the late, great John Candy was a big guy. The consequences are very comic.

Movies can do that occasionally, but they can't do it very often, because the camera is indeed usually a dispassionate viewpoint. Movies are comfortable having the dispassionate - or one might say, disinterested - camera as the viewpoint because the actors do so much of the work for the writer. Novels, though, which have no actors, tend to have a specific viewpoint in order to be emotionally effective.

When your readers read a novel they make an investment of emotion, time and money in it. Our time here on earth is limited. We're all going to pass on one day, and spending an evening reading a great novel (or seeing a great movie) is an excellent way of spending an evening, while an evening spent reading a crummy novel or seeing a bad movie is a lousy evening, which is a big reason for making your novel as good as possible. We have, after all, only a finite supply of evenings in our lives. And before you can start writing your novel and having a chance to make it live up to your readers' hopes and expectations, you need to choose a specific voice in which to tell your story.

What I know for certain is that the cinematic approach by and large does not work in novels. Dickens tries this in some parts of *Bleak House* (1853). About half the book is written ostensibly in the first-person and in the past tense by a character called Esther Summerson, and the rest features an omniscient, present-tense, mostly disinterested third-party narrator, who however never writes about Esther herself. The omniscient narrator tends to look at everybody rather like a movie camera might do.

However, you need to remember that by the time Dickens wrote *Bleak House* he was so famous that if he had written practically anything it would have been published. However, I don't recommend the use of the omniscient narrator to you. It can so easily seem pretentious and boring, and indeed I don't think Dickens is immune to these charges when he uses this kind of voice. I am afraid I consider *Bleak House* a seriously overrated novel, not in the same league as *Hard Times* (1854) or *Our Mutual Friend.*

Basically there are really only, at least in my view, two voices worth considering for a novel. The first is the first-person, which is quite a safe and sensible way to write a novel, particularly when it's your first. In fact, in his useful book *Writing a Novel* (1974), John Braine, author of *Room at the Top* (1957) - who did very well for himself with that first novel, which was written in the first-person - recommends the first-person for a first novel.

I don't think one should be that prescriptive, but certainly it's true that it's easier to write a novel in the first-person, as by and large I think if it's your first novel and you make it a first-person one it's more likely to get finished, than if you were writing a third-person novel.

The first-person viewpoint seems very natural. After all,

telling people a story about your life, at a dinner party for example, you would talk about yourself: 'Emma and I etc.'

Generally, it's probably easier to write a novel in the first-person than in the third-person. First-person novels aren't an automatic doddle to write, though. The main problem is obvious: the narrator is limited to what he or she or it (after all, it could be an animal or any inanimate object given imaginary life) perceives.

Also, by and large the narrator has to be there in the scene. You wouldn't get very far with writing your first-person novel where all you're doing is recounting what people have told you. 'John said it was a very exciting dinner party and afterwards they all took their clothes off and had lots of fun.' We actually want to be there (so to speak) with John as he experiences the scene rather than just listen to John telling the narrator about it!

You can use artificial devices to some extent when writing a first-person novel. Joseph Conrad, for example, frequently wrote narratives in the first-person within a third-person framework. The narrator (often a sailor called Charles Marlow) is basically telling a first-person story, though his narrative is effectively a first-person narrative inside the broader story. The way Conrad uses this technique, it does involve quite a lot of hearsay, but Marlow makes the other characters, who are telling him part of the story, interesting in their own right. Conrad employs this technique to very good effect in his novel *Lord Jim* (1899) which in effect allows the reader to piece together a chronicle and have the pleasure of feeling that only he, the reader, really knows the entirety of what happened to Jim, and so the reader becomes a kind of detective. *Lord Jim* is a sombre, powerful, difficult-to-forget masterpiece. But the technique is hard to get right, and Conrad himself was criticised in his own day for having a narrator (Marlow) whom the reader was expected to believe would be talking for more than six hours!

Conrad's famous novella *Heart of Darkness* (1899) features the technique being used in a more plausible way, if only because the book is much shorter and we can believe that Marlow could tell his story in the evening that is allocated to the telling. The story is a tale told by Marlow during an evening with some friends onboard a moored boat. It is typical of Conrad that no women are present while the story is being told. Also, *Heart of Darkness* is a more straightforward first-person narrative than *Lord Jim* and does not make such extensive use of other characters to tell the story.

By and large, if you're writing a first-person novel, I recommend that your narrator should be in every scene in some active way, even if (say) he or she is overhearing something taking place or is witnessing some action but not being seen.

There are particular opportunities for subtlety in first-person narration that are very much worth mentioning. One is where the narrator observes something whose significance we will understand at once, but where the narrator doesn't understand the significance, or at least not yet. This is normally possible where you have a narrator who is less knowledgeable about certain key matters - including human psychology - than the readers themselves. It can be a highly effective technique but is hard to get right, and should only be used if the technique has some direct relevance to an aspect of your story.

By the way, if you're writing a first-person novel, please don't imagine that the narrator must just be like you! That is a common mistake by inexperienced writers, and it often leads to them stuffing their novels with all sorts of personal stuff that may be of little or no interest to their readers. As I've already said, we want a story, not fragments of your autobiography. Don't let me stop you writing your autobiography if you really do want to write it, but an autobiography is not fiction anyway (or shouldn't be), and don't expect to find a mainstream publisher for it unless you're already famous or have had a really unusual and/or exciting life. After all, publishers want to make money, and they will know that few readers will buy your autobiography unless you're famous.

Instead, when writing your first-person novel, create an interesting character who will be the narrator, and accept that you need to reveal the character of the narrator as part of the process of unfolding your story.

Indeed, sometimes this gradual revelation of the nature of the character of the narrator will be a major, if not the most important, element of the story.

By the way, the narrator of a first-person novel does, on the whole, need to be fairly articulate. After all, he or she is telling a story. One of the problems, in my view, with John

Braine's novel *Room at the Top*, is that while certainly it's a good read, it's told by the narrator Joe Lampton, who is supposed to be an accountant for a local council, but who comes across as much more like a freelance writer than an accountant.

It's important to emphasise that your first-person narrator sometimes shouldn't know or see everything that you know or see as the author. (I suppose it's not ever possible for your first-person narrator to know or see *more* than the author knows or see.) As readers we like to infer conclusions for ourselves, and we enjoy encountering a first-person narrator who has obvious gaps in their knowledge. We like to fill in the gaps.

So a first-person narrator who doesn't spot everything can be very interesting. A first-person narrator who says, for example, 'I didn't really understand what was making her cry', when we the readers absolutely do understand that, emphasises the emotion of her crying and may give us sympathy for the narrator's emotional lack of insight (or blame him/her for it.). We will also feel more emotionally absorbed in the novel because we feel more of a participant in it.

A classic example of this kind of story is a novel that I've not actually read but which is regarded very highly. That is Kazuo Ishiguro's novel *The Remains of the Day* (1989) which has a narrator who is deliberately made to be emotionally obtuse and who does not notice things readers spot and who is emotionally cold and frigid as well. But that is rather a *tour de force* and for your first novel perhaps you shouldn't be that ambitious. *The Remains of the Day* was in fact Ishiguro's third published novel.

Another subtlety of using a first-person novel is where the narrator reports a clue to us which the narrator does not understand, but we do. If we suspect that we know more about the significance of the clue than the narrator knows, that will greatly add to the enjoyment the reader derives from the novel.

A first-person narrator, by the way, certainly cannot conceal things. I can't, for example, if I'm writing a novel about someone called Peter who is the narrator and who at the end of the story is thrown by the baddies onto a live rail on the London Underground but doesn't get killed because he's got an artificial plastic leg hidden under his trousers - well, you can't conceal the fact until that moment of him having the artificial leg which insulates him. If the reader doesn't already know that Peter's got an artificial leg, the reader is going to feel very, very cheated. The fact of his having an artificial leg needs to be mentioned earlier in the story, ideally in a fairly unobtrusive way, e.g. Peter might say, 'yes, I walk a bit stiffly because I lost my right leg when I was a kid in a road accident. I'm used to the artificial leg now and I don't think about it very much.' The mention of the artificial leg earlier in the story so that it won't be a complete surprise is called a 'plant'. Sometimes a plant will be a clue, of varying levels of subtlety that is picked up later. I look in detail at the concept of the plant in Chapter Seventeen.

You might ask: can one fluctuate between the first and third-person? A surprising - I should actually say alarming - proportion of novels submitted to Canterbury Literary Agency, have chapters written in the first-person and other chapters in the third-person.

I'll discuss the logic - or otherwise - for that creative choice in a moment, but I will say at once that I hate it and would *never* agent a book written in that way. The reader is surely entitled to ask, when presented with a novel which has both a first-person and third-person perspective, what on earth the actual voice of the novel is. Is the third-person narrator supposed to know about the first-person scenes? I'm not referring to a novel which is written in the third-person and which contains, say, some letters written in the first-person, as letters usually are, but rather a novel with specific individual passages and chapters written in the first-person along with passages and chapters written in the third-person.

Third-person narration involves telling the story in terms of 'he' or 'she' and what they did. It's also a fairly natural way of telling a story, though I do think the first-person voice is more natural. The third-person voice has the huge advantage over the first-person that you can take the reader into scenes in which the hero is not present. In Ken Follett's *Eye of the Needle*, for example, there are quite a few scenes where the 'Needle', the hero, is not actually present. Similarly, in the case of *The Day of the Jackal*, the story would not be possible without the third-person narrative because many of the scenes do not feature the Jackal at all.

Third-person narration is much more difficult than you might imagine. For one thing, it is hard to develop a third-person narrative voice where you can submerge your own personality enough to make the narration seem natural and neutral.

This problem, of the author intruding into the third-person narrative, is extremely common one in novels by inexperienced writers. I encounter this problem in submissions to Canterbury Literary Agency over and over again; indeed I would say on the whole that about nine out of ten submissions to the agency of sample material of novels in the third-person feature this problem: *the over-intrusive authorial narrator.*

Please remember: you are aspiring to write the novel *about* your characters and not about your own *opinion* of those characters.

This isn't a problem with the first-person narrative because you as author can't bring yourself into the story in the same way as you can with a third-person narrator. What you need to avoid doing when writing in the third-person is bringing in comments about your characters and about the action except on rare occasions where this is justified. Mostly, we really do not want those comments. We don't want to feel that you, the author, are the real main character of the story! After all, you have given your novel a title or are going to give it a title and the title is not, presumably, *My Thoughts About Life*, which so many third-person novels by inexperienced writers actually amount to being.

Here is an example of what I mean. It's a rather extreme example but not too extreme compared with many of the submissions made to the agency.

Francesca was a fine young woman; the kind of lady who wins any man's heart. As she skipped merrily down the road on the way to her first date, it would be difficult to imagine a more fetching example of an English rose.

That's very bad writing, but as I say it is by no means a far-fetched example. You see very clearly in this passage how the author's opinion dominates the whole material. We don't really get to know much about Francesca; but we do get to know a lot about the author and his or her attitude towards her.

The problem is that many writers in the past, including great writers like Dickens and George Eliot, *did* write in this authorially intrusive way and many of the people writing today have studied these classic novels when they were at school or university and assume that fiction can still be written like that today. Basically it can't.

There are several vital points to make here.

Firstly, you need to accept that the novel has evolved since the nineteenth century. While I'm not for a moment suggesting that Dickens or George Eliot are anything other than great exponents of the novel's art, technically their tendency on occasion to be too intrusive as authors is one of the weakest features of their work. They are fortunately brilliant at writing scenes with great dialogue and which are written as third-person scenes in novels should be written: that is, *from the perspective of a viewpoint character rather than with the author dominating the action.* So, for example, the Francesca passage ought to read something like this, which is admittedly not brilliant but it certainly shows how it should be done technically:

Francesca simply couldn't wait to see David. She wondered what he'd be wearing for their date and what the restaurant would be like. Looking up at the sky, and seeing its clear unbroken blue, she felt happier than she'd felt for ages. The prospect of the date with David felt so special she was giddy with the anticipation of it.

Again, that isn't necessarily brilliant but it does show you how you need to do things. Don't bring yourself into the story. Let the character's sensibility be what you're focusing on and in effect you, the author, need to become like the viewpoint character. There's nothing wrong with even setting down specific thoughts a viewpoint character has because they will help get the reader into the mind of that character.

In fact, what I tend to say to aspiring writers is that they should indeed write the story in the first-person if that is possible. As you develop your skills at writing fiction you will probably find yourself looking back in your early draft when you intruded into the action too much as an author and you will realise how far you've come and how much you've learned. For example, when I wrote the first draft of my novel *Josh Moonford and the Lost City of Cantia* (2019) which I began writing in April 2006, I wrote it in the third-person in a horribly authorially intrusive way, and while it had its amusing moments, my personality dominated the action and generally stopped the story from working. Fortunately I was lucky enough to get advice from the brilliant literary agent Russell Galen that I was writing in too intrusive a way. That was the first time I'd ever known that one shouldn't write fiction like this. I learnt a great deal from that advice Russell so kindly gave me and it transformed how I wrote fiction.

As it happens, I am much more comfortable writing in the first-person than in the third, but one novel I wrote as a ghost writer which has been published both in the UK and America is in the third-person and seems to work reasonably well. For reason of confidentiality I can't disclose the book's name.

One bizarre characteristic of George Eliot, who is undoubtedly one of the greatest writers in English of all time, and whose novel *Middlemarch* (1871) is one of the masterpieces of English literature, is that she frequently gives us a really great scene of dialogue and action and then feels it incumbent upon herself to spend about three or four pages commenting on what we've read and explaining what it means. She gets away with this because she's such a great writer and indeed, in all fairness, many of her comments about her characters are worth listening to, but it's still not what a novel should be doing. However, as I say, attitudes towards novel-writing have changed since the nineteenth century, partly influenced by movies, which of course do not allow for any authorial comment whatsoever.

In George Eliot's day, her general comments about her characters and about life were frequently extrapolated from her work and published in little subsidiary books, often by rival publishers, with the books being given feeble titles indicating that they contain wise sayings from George's Eliot's work. I hope she was paid royalties for these books.

So, when writing in the third-person *focus on the action and dialogue and get inside the mind of the viewpoint characters and don't start making comments about your characters; leave the judgment about the characters to be made by your readers.* If you follow that rule you should be fine.

Another vital point to make about third-person narrative is that you need a viewpoint character for every scene: that is, you need to view the action through the viewpoint of one particular character. You usually can't just use an omniscient narrator, that is, one who sees everything. It tends not to work. However, the omniscient third-person narrator can occasionally be used to comic effect e.g. 'And here this afternoon we see John Smith strolling happily up the drive of his home, his front door-key in hand, little imagining that right now, in his marital bedroom and not in the least expecting her husband's early return from his business trip, his devoted wife Mary Smith is succumbing, for the third time that afternoon, to the loving attentions of Mr Prendergast from next door but one.'

But generally choosing the omniscient third-person narrator as a device for writing an entire novel seems to me a mistake. Why? Because the remote, magisterial style tends to make the writing not very engaging emotionally.

Also, when you have a scene in your third-person novel featuring your hero, your hero or heroine must, by and large, be the viewpoint character. In *The Day of the Jackal* there are indeed lots of scenes where the Jackal doesn't actually appear but there's always a viewpoint character. In the scenes where he does appear, generally speaking he's the viewpoint character, though there are some exceptions to this.

For example, at one point the Jackal meets a beautiful French aristocratic lady in a hotel. They talk, flirt and he asks her to come to his room. At this point we switch to her viewpoint and see her downstairs wondering what to do, about whether to go to his room or not. Forsyth shows us that she feels lonely and wants to be told she's beautiful. Forsyth also tells us, through her viewpoint, that her husband is a base philanderer and always running off with young women, so we have enough reason to believe she's going to spend the night with the Jackal.

Towards the end of *The Day of the Jackal* there is a very interesting and dramatic scene where the detective Claude Lebel and the Jackal meet face-to-face. The viewpoint changes very dramatically. One moment it's the detective's viewpoint, then it's the viewpoint of a young policeman who is with the detective. So, yes, you can sometimes switch the viewpoint briefly, but that's not the same as constantly oscillating between too many characters' viewpoints. If you do that, your reader will have no idea which character to care about. As *How Not to Write a Novel* puts it, if you have too many viewpoints, you don't end up with a novel, but with a focus group.

A safe way of writing a third-person narrative is to make the main character the viewpoint character in every scene. This, of course, requires you to have your hero or heroine in every scene, much as in a first-person narrative. The fashion today is much more for that kind of approach. Those rather cinematic thrillers where in one scene it is, for example, *Monday, 9 am, Rio de Janeiro*, then in the next scene again for example it is *Monday 10 am, London*, nowadays seem rather dated, perhaps because movies do that sort of thing much better than novels and novelists are expected nowadays to create tension in their stories by more subtle methods.

It's actually much *easier* to write a third-person narrative from a particular character's viewpoint. Also, this approach tends to make the scene more emotionally coherent and engaging.

I've already mentioned Martin Cruz Smith's *Gorky Park*, which is also an excellent film with a superb screenplay by the late, great Dennis Potter. *Gorky Park* is a third-person novel but Arkady Renko, the investigator, is pretty much always the viewpoint character. You could probably convert *Gorky Park* into a first-person novel quite easily, because it's very much happening in Arkady Renko's head.

I myself feel that *Gorky Park* is a more emotionally compelling novel than, say, *The Day of the Jackal* or *Eye of the Needle*, partly because we spend more of it inhabiting the head of the main character. And I'd again emphasise that using this focused approach makes it easier to tell the story. When there are a lot of different viewpoints it does make the story more disjointed. The craft of novel-writing, like all crafts, evolves.

In a writers' club, and indeed some published writers do this too, writers often produce more complex types of narration. One popular example is that alternate chapters are narrated by different characters in the first-person.

I personally feel that this is a device that doesn't really work. It always seems slightly insincere, rather like these newscasts from America where we get a cute male and a cute female sharing the newscasting assignment together. Having multiple first-person narrators in a novel is an intellectually respectable technique - Nobel Prize winning novelist William Faulkner used it, for example, in his novel *The Sound and the Fury* (1929) - but I still don't like it. First-person and third-person narrative is, after all, a natural way of telling a story, and multiple first-person narratives isn't.

Occasionally people try to write books in the *second person*: Jay McInerney's successful novel *Bright Lights, Big City* (1984) is written in this way, but it seems to me an unsatisfactory technique, though I rather enjoyed that book, and also the movie, which I saw in New York soon after it came out. After all, if the reader reads a sentence such as e.g. 'you flew to New York that morning and caught a yellow cab to the Bronx Zoo' (I've just made this up; it isn't from the novel), the reader could always respond, 'no I didn't!'

When you've got your first novel published you can then be more ambitious and experimental, if you really want to be, but I recommend you simply focus on telling a great story. Don't let me stop you experimenting once you're established, though. It's all very well Picasso doing his Cubism with people whose eyes are dangling around their cheeks, but before he did that he had painted many masterpieces in a much more conventional manner.

And if you don't think you can write in the first-person? Well, if that's how you feel then don't do it. Many writers feel that some narrative voices are beyond them. Norman Mailer once said that after reading E. M. Forster in the third-person, he, Mailer, could only write in the first-person. On the other hand I myself like creating a character and inhabiting that character and I find that easier to do when I'm writing in the first-person rather than the third.

Part of me, by the way, feels that a third-person narrative is inherently flawed when you are writing a children's book. Why? Because children's books are written by adults, not by children. It's very hard for an adult to avoid condescension towards the children. True, J. K. Rowling, an instinctively brilliantly talented writer, manages to do this in her Harry

Potter stories. She avoids talking about the characters in a condescending or a patronising way.

Something you must also especially strive to avoid, by the way, if you're doing a third-person narration about children, is what is sometimes called 'chubby fistery', where you're being patronising to them. Don't say, for example, 'little Mark held the rattle in his chubby fist.' You really can't say things like that. You also can't do what one of my agency's writers did before I edited it out - that was a blip really, the book is pretty good - where, in his third-person narrative, he used the phrase 'like all eleven year olds...' You can't write like that! After all, when we were children we did not think of ourselves as inferior adults and indeed we weren't. We were possibly superior to adults. We thought of ourselves as entities, deserving respect in our own right, and we were!

Anybody who wants to write for children with an aim of talking down to them, or who believes that their views and feelings are not as important as those of adults, or not in fact often more so, is most likely never going to write successfully for children. Yes, we can look back at when we were children and when we believed or thought things which we may not believe or think now, and perhaps some of our childhood enthusiasm seems rather naïve in retrospect. But why should we be any more ashamed of feeling like that as children, than of some of the jaded attitudes to life we may have as adults? I think we should be proud of having been children and accept that their perspective is as good as anybody else's and in fact may be better, because they're often more emotionally honest than adults. And frequently better people, too. For example, as far as I'm aware, no child has ever begun any world war.

You'll quite rightly deduce from the above that, as I've suggested, telling a story in the third-person *and* in the first-person in the same book can't possibly work. It's silly and totally confusing for the reader. Let *Bleak House* be the last book that does it.

All right, now let's talk about the scenes you decide should be in your story.

11. Which scenes should be in your story?

How many scenes should you have in your novel and how do you choose which scenes to include?

A well-known London literary agent once said to me, and it was good advice, that a novel should consist of about fifty scenes.

So if we have the fifty-scene rule in mind, how do we decide what scenes you use to tell it? The answer is the *significant* scenes. Those are the scenes the reader needs to care about to absorb and enjoy your story. Deciding this is never easy, but if you care about your story and are professional, which means sticking to that story, and avoiding irrelevant digressions, you should before long be able to work out which scenes to use.

If you look at most recent DVDs of major Hollywood movies they often have, in the Special Features section, a short film about making the movie. It's useful to watch these little films: you realise how much work goes into the screenplay and into the actual process of story-telling and also just how many scenes are filmed and then cut out of the film during the edit.

After you've got your first draft finished you'll almost certainly spot scenes that need taking out. I remember a producer saying in the short film about making the blockbuster *Gladiator*, 'you often think something's essential and it's not.' Indeed, when making *Gladiator*, they spent a lot of money, more than a million pounds, because they got obsessed with wanting to have a rhinoceros in the amphitheatre. With the greatest respect to rhinoceroses, they are rather unintelligent animals and pretty much impossible to train. So the producers of the movie decided to make a completely digital rhinoceros and it cost them about a million pounds to do this and they got truly obsessed by it and in the end they thought, we don't want this in the film anyway. That kind of thing happens when novels are being written too.

The first scene in your novel should be the first vital one. I can't tell you how to start a novel. It depends what your novel needs, but I do know that if you can't think of a scene that figuratively arrests your reader from the word go, your reader may not be around to read the rest of your scenes.

The Day of the Jackal has a masterly start. It begins with the following sentence:

It is cold at six forty in the morning of a March day in Paris, and seems even colder when a man is about to be executed by firing squad.

It's about the real-life execution of a fellow called Bastien-Thiry, who was a chief plotter in an assassination attempt on De Gaulle. Jean Bastien-Thiry's execution in the novel leads to the organisation that wanted to kill De Gaulle abandoning the job itself and instead hiring a professional killer, the Jackal, to try to carry out the mission. That's of course where Forsyth mixes facts and fiction.

But that's just one way of beginning a book. David Lodge begins his novel *Nice Work*, which is about an industrialist and an academic falling in love, very differently. It starts like this:

Monday, January 13 1986. Victor Wilcox lies awake, in the dark bedroom, waiting for his quartz alarm clock to beep.

A professional always starts with something dramatic in the context of the story. A big part of the story of *Nice Work* focuses on Vic's angst about his career and personal relationships, so to have him waking up in the dark and feeling anxious is a pretty good way for the book to start.

The Day of the Jackal, on the other hand, is a political thriller and crime thriller combined and starting with an execution on a steely cold day in Paris makes sense.

To emphasise this main point again, *we don't need to know things or see scene, unless they are relevant to the story*. If they are not relevant to the story we don't need them. Every scene should advance the story significantly or it shouldn't be in the book. You don't need to reveal everything, though. Readers enjoy having things to work out for themselves and finding things out without having everything spelled out to them.

Which raises the interesting question of how you handle *backstory*.

12. Backstory

Backstory is what a character has done before we meet them.

Backstory is crucially important to us in our lives. Our backstories are, in a very real sense, who we are from the moment we're born up to just now.

At professional level, there is a name for our backstories: our CVs.

When we meet new people, a big part of our conversation with them will focus on their backstory. The presence of backstory is something we expect and its absence makes us uncomfortable. You are hardly likely to offer a job to someone, who is say, forty-five, and who tells you they have never had a job in their life. Nor, if you go on a date and meet someone in their thirties or forties or older who says, 'I've never had a relationship. This is my first date in my whole life,' you might not be confident that this is a very normal person, let alone someone with whom you might want to have a relationship. On the one hand nor do you want her or him to say, 'I still love Jeremy/Jemima. No-one could match him/her.' That's not very auspicious either.

So backstory is vitally important to us.

Using backstory in a novel is a challenge and not an easy one to get right.

Here's what you *can't* do. You can't just give an info-dump, where you just splurge all the backstory out. That would be like going to a party, meeting a new person, and then they spend half an hour telling you all about their life so far. Unless they're *very* attractive, and you're very single, you're unlikely to be impressed, and even if you are, what is there left to get to know after they've told you so much already?

So, how should you present this backstory information? One way of doing it is through a scene which shows the character engaged in doing whatever his or her backstory chronicles.

Otherwise, backstory needs 'trickling' into the story at crucial moments. This trickling in of the backstory is an absolute hallmark of the novelist who knows what they're doing. After all, don't we trickle in our backstories when we meet someone new? Anyone who, when they met a stranger, just blurted out their back story to them would seem a bit weird, after all.

Back in the early part of the twentieth century, the novelists Joseph Conrad and Ford Madox Ford, who were friends and who collaborated on some novels, earnestly discussed the nature of fiction. According to Ford, in his 1924 book *Joseph Conrad: A personal rememberance* '*we agreed that the general effect of a novel must be the general effect that life makes upon mankind*' (my italics).

I think this a momentous and major remark, and very much worth ingraining into the fibre of your writing brain. It explains why so much of the craft of fiction involves in effect mastering techniques that will help you, when you write your novel, to imitate the effect that life has on people. That is what you should be doing in your fiction. So, to take just one example, as we don't do info-dumps in life, why should we do them in the novels we write?

After all, the novel is not some sort of rarefied art form, it is part of life. It comes out of life and the same rules apply to someone telling you an anecdote at a dinner party or someone telling you a story anywhere else that would apply to writing a novel.

In *The Day of the Jackal*, Frederick Forsyth expertly dishes out small, tasty dollops of backstory to convey the menace of the Jackal, who is a ruthless professional killer. Here is the first time we encounter the Jackal in the novel.

As he [Marc Rodin] boarded his train a Comet 4B of BOAC drifted down the flight path towards Runway Zero-Four at London Airport. It was inbound from Beirut. Among the passengers as they filed through the arrivals lounge was a tall, blond Englishman. His face was healthily tanned by the Middle Eastern sun. He felt relaxed and fit after two months enjoying the undeniable pleasures of the Lebanon and the, for him, even greater pleasure of supervising the transfer of a handsome sum of money from a bank in Beirut to another in Switzerland. Far behind him on the sandy soil of Egypt, long since buried by the baffled and furious Egyptian police, each with a neat bullet hole through the spine, were the bodies of two German missile engineers. Their departure from life had set back the development

of Nasser's Al Zafira rocket by several years and a Zionist
millionaire in New York felt his money well spent. After
passing easily through Customs the Englishman took a hire
car to his flat in Mayfair.

I don't believe anyone could reasonably claim that *The
Day of the Jackal* is a literary masterpiece, because literary
masterpieces make you feel wondrously moved by the
human condition, and ultimately *The Day of the Jackal*
does not, I think, have that effect on us. All the same,
it's a book written with great literary skill in the art of
holding the reader's interest, and we get a very good
view in the passage I've just quoted of how Frederick
Forsyth does this. He has the clearest idea of what his
anti-hero is like, and there is a sense of urgency about how
Forsyth communicates to his reader the world of the hired
assassin. In just one paragraph, one that tells us what the
'tall, blond Englishman' has been doing in Beirut, we
learn that the Englishman kills people for a living. We
understand tacitly that the assassin does not have the
least sympathy for his victims, or is likely to spend even
an instant in feeling guilty about what he's done. Notice
how we are immediately invited to sympathise with the
Jackal, rather than with the two missile engineers, who
are portrayed as having been up to no good, anyway.

The calmness, efficiency, and deadliness of the Jackal
are all emphasised, and during the book Forsyth regularly
mentions the Jackal's enjoyment of the luxurious lifestyle
his success brings him. There are several quite detailed

accounts of meals the Jackal enjoys, and the lavish accommodation he occupies in the hotels rooms he favours is also frequently emphasised. We only see him with one woman in the book, but she is a beautiful French aristocrat and she enjoys her liaison with this calm, handsome and potent man until, inevitably, she is herself murdered by him for having learnt the truth about his mission. The efficiency and economy of the Jackal's backstory is handled very well indeed.

So he's a handsome man who kills for a living. Is that all we get to know about the Jackal's backstory? No, not quite. We get another little glimpse, too, in a crucial scene where the Jackal learns that his cover has been blown, that he will now be hunted by the police, and that he faces a stark choice: continue with his mission and try to complete it in the face of significant odds, or return the first part of his fee and abandon the mission.

Will Osborne's comment on this section made me realise that I hadn't mentioned enough in the first draft about how important escapism is in how Forsyth portrays the Jackal. Certainly, writing primarily for an audience in the UK that had, at least in the nineteen sixties when the book came out (it was written in 1967) relatively drab lives, Forsyth quite reasonably plays up the lifestyle escapism factor of the Jackal's life for all it's worth, and does it very well. On this matter Will comments *'Don Simpson, producer of many films including "Top Gun" once said to me in a meeting, as a callow ingenue. "We are not in the film* business, we're in the transportation business" meaning literally he saw his job as to transport audiences in the cinema from their own lives to other worlds comprising wish fulfillment.' I wouldn't agree the transportation is always about wish fulfillment, it can be about many other things, but I would agree wholeheartedly that the transportation of the audience's mindset, and indeed souls, is vitally important, and ultimately at the heart of what a movie does for its audience.

Of course as readers we want the Jackal to continue with his plan, but we need to feel convinced of the reasons why he makes his choice. Not surprisingly, perhaps, it's money that makes him want to proceed. Yet the matter is more subtle than that; the Jackal realises that giving up now means risking all his quality of life, and everything he has achieved so far.

Faced with the knowledge that the police are now looking for an assassin they know has been hired to kill De Gaulle, even if they don't know about the Jackal's precise false identities, the Jackal, weighing up in his mind what to do, is finally decisively influenced by getting the bill from the luxurious café where he has been having a pot of coffee on a terrace of an ultra-smart hotel on the French Riviera. Should he give up his mission, return the down-payment and slink away, or should he continue? The passage in which he makes his decision is so good it is worth setting down in full.

The bill came; he glanced at it and winced. *God, the prices these people charged! To live this kind of life a man needed to be rich, to have dollars, and dollars and even more dollars. He looked out at the jewelled sea and the lithe brown girls walking along the beach, the hissing Cadillacs and snarling Jaguars that crept along the Croisette, their bronzed young drivers keeping half an eye on the road and the other flicking along the pavements for a likely pick-up. This was what he had wanted for a long time, from the days when he had pressed his nose to the travel agent's window and gazed at the posters showing another life, another world, far from the drudgery of the commuter train and the forms in triplicate, the paper clips and tepid tea. Over the past three years he had almost made it; a glimpse here, a touch there. He had got used to good clothes, expensive meals, a smart flat, a sports car, elegant women. To go back meant to give it all up.*

We see that The Jackal understands that in the decision he is about to make, the pupose of his entire life is at stake he is on his way to his rendezvous with destiny.

How does one write as well as this? Well, first of all Forsyth clearly knows the Jackal's character very well. Also, you need talent and a facility for expressing a character's thoughts in words, but after all, none of us are (probably) born with an innate literary ability; it's something we need to learn.

Additionally, to use backstory well you need to be assured in your use of the skill of letting the backstory trickle in, and ideally to make the trickling in happen when the insertion of the nugget of backstory has maximum dramatic impact and/or relevance to the plot. After all, Forsyth could have already told us about the Jackal's days of poverty and obscurity, when the Jackal wanted a life more glamorous than he'd had then. Yes, Forsyth could have told us about that earlier, but how much more effective to tell us about it now, at this absolutely crucial moment in the story!

To use backstory well you need to know your characters and care about them. And that means, from the outset, choosing characters you find deeply interesting even if you don't necessarily like them.

They don't all need to be goodies, of course, nor indeed should they be. Many of the greatest characters in literature, from Richard III in Shakespeare's play of the same name, to Satan in *Paradise Lost* onwards, are baddies rather than goodies, but we like them all the same, maybe because they allow us to indulge fantasies we may have of behaving amorally sometimes without anyone getting hurt. One reason we like the Jackal, surely, is because he lets us enjoy the vicarious pleasure of being ruthless, murderous, sexually irresistible etc. etc. without necessarily needing to handle the consequences if we actually were all those things.

13. Choosing your characters

It certainly makes sense to write about characters who you want to write about so much that you can't *not* write about them. After all, you're going to be spending a year on your novel, and maybe much longer. You may as well spend it with characters you like and care about.

Don't, by the way, make your characters too perfect. After all, again to refer you to life, no-one is too perfect. On the other hand, the reader needs to have some basic liking for the character. Also, the character, even if really bad, has to be to some extent attractive.

Hannibal Lecter, in the novel *The Silence of the Lambs* (1988) and the 1991 movie of the same name, likes eating people generally and their inner organs in particular, but he is attractive because he's cultured, polite, fair-minded, (he doesn't kill you if he finds the world more interesting with you in it, so we'd better all make sure we're interesting), and he is not actually physically unattractive.

So make your characters interesting by giving them certain strong characteristics. If you write about a character you find interesting, you are likely to be able to convey that interest to your reader. But, again, don't make the character too much like you; after all, it's a novel you're writing, not an autobiography.

Next, write about people, and situations and settings, you know about both technically and emotionally. I think *The Mating Game* works reasonably well as a novel because my co-author Jovanka Houska and I know about the world of chess and what goes on in it.

However, you don't need to confine yourself to what you know about literally. No, use your imagination. I very much doubt J.K. Rowling has ever done a *genuine* magic spell, but she writes about magical people (and non-magical ones) brilliantly. If you only write about what you literally know about that's going to limit your fiction-writing, because writers tend to be relatively sedentary people who are often at happiest at their desk writing, and who don't necessarily want to do stuff that other people find so necessary such as climbing Everest, doing lots of travelling, attending demonstrations, doing a charity bungee jump etc.

Besides, your *emotional* knowledge of situations and things is more important for your writing than your literal knowledge of them. The secret is to make the most imaginatively of what you've experienced emotionally. For example, when J.K. Rowling writes so well about those ghastly creatures the Dementors, it's obvious she associates them with the worst times she's had in her life, and she uses that knowledge to make them emotionally perfectly convincing in their ghastliness. To take an example from the work of a less well-known writer, viz me, my Young Adult novel *Josh Moonford and the Lost City of Cantia* is set in a weird underground world, Cantia, underneath

Canterbury. Clearly, I can't know anything literally about that, but I do think I know about it emotionally. I used to live in Finland and I often felt pretty alienated there, even though I learnt to speak the language. I'm quite sure I used those feelings of alienation when I wrote about Cantia. I personally only tend to write about settings that I've actually been to or know about, or feel I can imagine.

A good writer doesn't need much experience on which to base a novel. Joseph Conrad's *Nostromo* (1904) for all its sometimes slightly tedious way of being written, is unquestionably a masterpiece, full of life, action and colour. Conrad only visited Venezuela for about four days prior to writing *Nostromo* (he wrote it some years after his visit) - and this was his only ever landfall in South America - but he created a highly convincing South American country and town in the novel. I think he knew South America well emotionally, and that this enabled him to write the book.

I tend to believe that writers should follow the rule that if they haven't actually been to a literal place they shouldn't write about it, because they probably can't do so effectively. I've lived in Finland, I've lived in Germany, I've spent quite a lot of time in France and on the East Coast and West Coast of the United States, I could probably set novels in those places with a reasonable hope of making the writing realistic. I'm not going to set a novel in India or Thailand or Borneo (to give just three examples) as I've never been to those places. If I really had to do it I would actually try and keep the scene very short and I would try and convey the unfamiliarity of being there in the viewpoint.

The novel is not an opportunity for someone to just experiment, it's an opportunity to tell a convincing story and so you need to know about your settings both physically and emotionally.

So how do we convey a sense of place, or location, in fiction? Well, yes, my advice is again, by and large, to be relatively impressionistic in how we do it. We don't want an encyclopaedic description of a setting.

After all, YouTube has videos of pretty much every place on the planet. What you can offer, as a novelist, is what it *feels* like to be there. Many Victorian novels start with extensive descriptions of the physical setting. It's almost part of the deal of writing a Victorian novel that you have to do that. But nowadays we haven't got so much time for reading that kind of description and in any case if you want such detailed accounts of a place why not buy a travel guide rather than the novel?

Yes, writing about things you know about emotionally is essential. I would not write about drug dealers, well, not very much anyway: *The Mating Game* does contain a page or two about two of them. I think I could imagine drug dealers but I don't know them emotionally and also I wouldn't want to write about drug dealers at any length. When, in *Josh Moonford and the Lost City of Cantia* I write about two cockney villains, I depict them as slightly comic and based them on some of the people I knew in Leicester (I grew up there). I think it worked reasonably well. I don't really know any cockneys, but imagining they were from Leicester did seem to work OK, though I did give them cockney rhyming slang.

Now let's look at writing about villains.

Will: *'The worst advice, in my opinion, is that old canard "write what you know", as it completely closes down your imagination and suggests that you write about your own life and experiences which, unless you have lived an extraordinary life, is likely to be mundane and quotidian.'*

14. Depicting villains

In good novels and good movies, villains tend to exult in their villainy. You especially find this in movies, but the technique works in prose fiction too. Hannibal Lecter, for example, exults in his villainy in a rather subtle way in Thomas Harris's brilliant thriller *The Silence of the Lambs.*

Villains should ideally be larger than life and at least to some extent fun to read about. A useful way to make them come across like this is indeed to show them enjoying being villains. Thomas Harris frequently refers to Hannibal Lecter having fun doing the dark things he does. Villains in literature often do have fun in the sense that they enjoy being villains. Another memorable example of a villain enjoying being a villain occurs in the movie *Cliffhanger* (1993) a thriller starring Sylvester Stallone. The actor John Lithgow gives a great performance as the villain Eric Qualen. Lithgow really hams it up, yet never so much that you cease to find him believable. At one point, for example, he says, 'You'd like to kill me, wouldn't you, Tucker? Well take a ticket and get in line!' And it's wonderful because we see he's aware that he's evil and he enjoys being evil. That's not only Eric Qualen's prerogative. You get it in *Paradise Lost* (1667) too. Satan, the villain of *Paradise Lost*, very much enjoys being evil. Half the best lines of *Paradise Lost* are spoken by the baddies. One of the best lines is spoken by Satan. It is, 'Not to know me argues yourselves unknown', meaning that we all have the potential for wickedness inside us. That's what Satan thinks, anyway. I don't know if he's right or not, but if he is, it might explain why we find villainy entertaining, or perhaps we can simply enjoy the idea of villainy without needing to feel the horrible sense of guilt that committing wicked acts in reality would make us feel.

Will: *'The best villains as in life are the ones who don't think they're villains.'*

15. Dialogue

Let's talk about dialogue.

Dialogue is a challenge for all writers. Dialogue makes or mars a novel. When I was beginning to try and write fiction, about forty years ago, my dialogue was pretty bad. I think I've got it better now, but there are always new things to learn about dialogue.

A novel is not a snapshot of real life, it's a story where everything in it should be significant. The same is true of dialogue. If someone said, 'What dialogue should go into a novel?' I'd say, only the dialogue that's significant for the story.

Yes, we do need to have occasional social chit-chat dialogue, because the dialogue has to be realistic and social chit-chat is a part of life. But basically you need to get down to action pretty soon. Remember the rule about how screenplay writers should get into the scene as late as they can and leave it as soon as they can? It's great advice. So only put dialogue in that you actually need.

Good dialogue should obey the following rules. First of all, it should be capable of being spoken aloud. A good test of dialogue is whether you can read it aloud. Secondly, you don't need whole sentences in the dialogue. After all, we don't usually speak in whole sentences. We don't tend to do long speeches, either.

In real-life dialogue we also tend to talk in fairly short bursts. In novels, too, dialogue is better when it's shorter. A lot of dialogue in Victorian novels is terribly wordy, partly because most Victorian novelists had not really mastered dialogue. Novel-writing was still only fifty or sixty years old. Dickens's dialogue is normally very good, but even he is too wordy sometimes, or uses words that the character wouldn't use.

By the way, make sure you use elision in your dialogue. We do not usually say, for example, 'I will be there tomorrow,' but 'I'll be there tomorrow.' If you don't use elision your dialogue can seem terribly stilted. Remember that dialogue seeks to set down on the page how people speak, while leaving out (most of) the 'ums and ers' and general repetitions that people generate when they really speak. Any spoken language is very different from written language. You can use one-word sentences in dialogue, and any other technique that makes your dialogue seem natural and realistic.

By the way, many inexperienced prose fiction writers put internal dialogue - what characters are thinking - in speech marks. Only use speech marks, please, if something is actually said aloud. Otherwise, use italics, although with practice, you'll discover you can often dispense with italics for all your characters' thoughts and just use italics for the emphasised parts. For example (I am not using italics throughout for this example to avoid confusion):

John watched Helen gyrate on the dance floor. I wonder what it'd be like to have a date with her? he thought. *Even better, what would a night with her be like?*

16. What kind of prose should you be writing?

Let's now move on to thinking about the kind of prose you should be aiming for.

There's often a feeling among inexperienced fiction writers that leads to them thinking rather like this: 'I'm engaged on a literary endeavour, therefore I should be literary in my style.'

Please don't let yourself think like that: it's a big mistake.

In fact the kind of prose you need to write is whatever will tell your story in the clearest, most concise fashion, using words that are neither especially 'literary' or 'non-literary' but simply most fit for the purpose of telling the story. The idea of a novel being a story told around a camp-fire is, I think, again useful here because in fact the test of good prose, like good dialogue, is that it can be read out. I think the best kind of prose fiction writing is the writing you don't notice because you're so absorbed in the story.

Ultimately, the only way you can learn to write clear, concise prose and natural-sounding dialogue is through lots of practice that is constantly complemented by a desire to give the reader a good time. After all, as I've said earlier, the reader is your customer. So your novel is essentially your shop, and if you were running a shop, wouldn't you want your customers to enjoy being there and to find things there that they like?

17. Plants

Let's now talk about plants. Because a plant is very important in fiction, just as in a garden.

Plants are apparently insignificant details that become significant in the plot later on. They require careful judgement to devise and to insert into your story in a subtle way that plays fair with the reader and gives him or her a chance to notice the plant but avoids drawing excessive attention to it.

For example, imagine if in your novel there's a fish tank in the villain's living room, in which he keeps a number of goldfish and also a cone shell - some cone shells happen to have an extremely virulent poison - which the villain is going to use to kill a victim at some point.

You could introduce this plot idea by writing something like:

John took a step towards the aquarium: 'Please excuse me for a moment. I have to feed the fish.'

And he drops some fish food in the tank, and maybe one of his guests asks him what fish he has in there, and he mentions a few names of fish, and then says there are some interesting and unusual shellfish too.

If we find later on that he uses one of these shellfish to kill his victim, we will accept that. We won't feel cheated. What you can't do is, near the end of your novel, have the police say to John when John is being interrogated:

'Our lab people say that Mr Brown was killed by some sort of fish poison.' John gave a nod of grudging acceptance, then said: 'Since you know so much already, I am going to tell you everything. He deserved it. He cheated with my wife when they were both a business conference last month. A cone shellfish I brought three years ago and keep in my aquarium possesses one of the most virulent poisons of any shellfish in the world. I used that to kill that creep Brown.'

You can't take the reader by suprise like that with a plant that's never been mentioned before. The reader thinks, *I didn't know about the aquarium. It's not fair. It's cheating.* And the reader would be right. It's a very unnecessary form of cheating, because you could have just put the plant in earlier on.

But don't make a plant too obvious. In the Columbo series of detective programmes, the stories usually have a plant but it is sometimes very clumsily done. In one episode a young playboy explains that his parents were killed some years ago 'in a freak explosion'. This young playboy (acted very well by Roddy McDowall) is fairly creepy anyway and once he mentions how his parents died, we don't have the slightest doubt he's the murderer.

But not all plants are designed to present the reader

with a useful and often hardly-noticeable clue which will acquire a great deal of resonance later in the story. Sometimes the plant can be more subtle than this and have a tremendously powerful impact, given that the reader or audience member notices it.

There is a good example of this in James Cameron's brilliant movie *Titanic* (2000) which he both wrote and directed. Incidentally, if ever you find yourself despairing of writing something really good, try to get hold of an early draft of his screenplay for *Titanic* and notice how enormously different - and, frankly, much worse - it is than the final film. Good screenplays and good novels tend not to be written but re-written, and arguably for most writers the real work only begins once the first draft has been completed.

But if you've never written a novel or a screenplay before, take consolation from the fact that once you have finished that first draft, the process of editing and improving is much easier and less stressful than writing that first draft and indeed is extremely enjoyable.

Will: *'The thing that excellent novels and excellent films share is good editing.'*

Quite early on in *Titanic,* not long after the Jack character played by Leonardo di Caprio has met the heroine Rose, played by Kate Winslet, Rose asks Jack about his past and discovers that he spent time in Paris using his artistic skills to draw people he encountered in the city. One of these people, and Jack tells Rose quite a lot about her, is an old lady dressed in her best who spends her evenings in a bar in her finery dressed as she did when she was young because she is mourning the death or disappearance of a man she loved years ago and has never got over him. This is a very clever plant because when we first hear about that, especially if this is the first time we have seen the film, we don't think any more of it other than that Jack is simply telling Rose about someone he knew in Paris. But we discover much later in the film - and I think the movie was released long enough ago for there to be a fair chance that you have already seen it, but if you haven't please don't read the rest of this paragraph - that Rose loses Jack and while the whole point of the ending of the film is that Jack's love and loyalty inspired Rose to have an extremely full life, she did spend the rest of her life mourning him even though in her full life she married someone else and had children and grandchildren.

The point is that this kind of plant can offer a wonderful artistic resonance to a story although in all fairness I very much doubt that people would pick up on this particular plant until they've seen *Titanic* on several occasions, which I have and I never cease to find the movie delightful.

Coming back to prose fiction, there are some extremely ingenious and highly effective plants in Anthony Burgess's masterpiece *Earthly Powers* (1980): a remarkable and lengthy novel which is essentially a fictitious autobiography of a writer recounting his life through his eight decades and which takes in most of the significant events in the world, the early twentieth century to about the 1970s.

There are two particular types of plants in *Earthly Powers* I want to mention here.

Firstly there is one rather like the plant in *Titanic*; it only acquires full resonance later in the story. Fairly early on in the story the narrator Kenneth Toomey has a bizarre dream in which his sister Hortense is blinded in an eye during an accident. We think no more of this dream until later in the book we discover that Hortense - who works in metal sculpture - has indeed had an accident which has cost her one eye.

The narrator doesn't remark on his dream when he hears about Hortense's terrible accident, and we are given the impression that perhaps he himself has forgotten about the dream, although it is unlikely that we have. I've often wondered what Burgess is saying here. I think he might be suggesting that people may sometimes in certain circumstances have an ability to predict the future.

There is another, highly ingenious and entertaining plant in *Earthly Powers* when Toomey is kidnapped by the Nazis while in Germany at the outbreak of the World War 2, trying to rescue a Jewish writer whose work he loves. Unfortunately the rescue doesn't work because the Nazis capture the Jewish writer and they also capture Toomey. However, because the Nazis regard Toomey as fairly harmless he is given a straightforward deal - this echoes the deal that the writer P. G. Wodehouse was himself given in reality when captured by the Nazis while living in France at the outbreak of war. Toomey is offered his freedom in exchange for taking part in an amicable radio discussion about Britain and Germany. The Nazis promise that Toomey does not need to say anything excessively incriminating but can basically say what he wants as long as it is not blatantly anti-Nazi.

The reader is given the full text of the interview and this interview includes a sequence in which Toomey offers an apparently innocuous message for the Nazis that appears to be a rather bland expression of the need for collaboration and amiability between nations. Here is an extract from the text of the interview which includes the passage I want to focus on:

In this scene, Toomey is being interviewed by a Nazi who speaks with a decidedly upper-class British accent when he speaks English. The first person speaking here is Toomey and his interviewer is the Nazi:

'... Meanwhile, the rest of us can at least pray that peace will soon come again.'

'Amen to that, Mr Toomey. If I may ask you a general question, what do you consider to be the finest thing in life?'

'Marcus Aurelius put it rather well, I think. He said: "For us creatures, knowledge that heaven exists beatifies life - "'

'Very beautiful, Mr Toomey.'

'"- Or opens doors yielding noble action. Zeal inspires sanctity."'

'Have you a message for both the German and the British peoples?'

'Yes. May all your hearts in the long eras rolling

relentlessly on teach innocence, not hate. Everyone - 'Yes,
Mr Toomey?'
   'Learn love.'
   'Thank you, Mr Toomey.'
   The red light went out.

On the face of it Toomey has simply given some bland, touchy-feely comment about his desire for peaceful co-existence between Nazi Germany and Britain at a time when Britain has just launched a war against an evil power. But later in the novel, during a tribunal hearing which Toomey has to face after his return to Britain where various members of the secret services, while not exactly furious with him, challenge him about what he was doing, Toomey reveals that on the face of it the bland message was in fact an acrostic and that if you take the first letter of every word of his message a rather less bland message for the Nazis is revealed, viz. 'May Hitler rot in hell'. The other acrostic in the passage is more blunt: 'F*** the bloody Nazis.'

By the time Anthony Burgess wrote *Earthly Powers* he was one of the finest novelists writing in English and in many ways his great novel is a kind of compendium of his brilliant attitude towards story-telling and using language, but ultimately he's not giving anything so spectacularly difficult to emulate in setting down these plants; he is simply doing what every professional novelist should be doing: that is, aiming to do his very best to give the reader a great time.

Another plant I really like occurs in the first *Back to the Future* film where the only reason Marty keeps the flyer poster which has a vitally important picture of the stopped clock on it is because his girlfriend writes her phone number on the back of the poster. It is vital that he has that poster for the plot so that he knows what time the clock stops once he travels back to 1955. The first *Back to the Future* film is full of ingenious plants that add greatly to the pleasure of anyone watching the film.

Will: *'This is similar to the screenwriting rule of set up and pay off. Try to make a good percentage of events that are set up in the earlier part of the story get paid off later in the story. Simple things like perhaps a sense of smell, or taste, that later helps or saves our hero as an example.'*

18. Making your novel more real than reality

I remember years ago reading some book about advice to writers. One of the illuminating points it made, is that some children had put on a play at school and the play had been evaluated by a dramatic adviser, who said it was a good play, but that the brother and sister in the play didn't look like brother and sister. The children thought this comment hilarious. 'But they're brother and sister in real life!' they exclaimed. Yet the adviser said, 'that may be the case but my comment is still valid.' The advisor was right, and this is very revealing about the nature of art.

It's a bit like saying, 'that really happened'. But saying that something really happened is no defence; it still needs to work and seem plausible as art. Even though they were brother and sister in real life, the adviser's comment that, in the context of the play they did not look like a brother and sister is still a valid one, because you are creating art, and art is not real life. 'It really happened,' is a defence in real life, but not in art.

Think of the things in real life that are amazing. You would hardly dare to put them in a novel, because people wouldn't believe you. An English-speaking enclave in

Spain? An American air base in Cuba? A Spanish town in Morocco? You can hardly believe such places exist, yet they do. Do you know that in 1864 a cable was laid from New York to Cornwall underneath the Atlantic Ocean, by putting a 3,000 mile cable onto a boat and then just unfurling it? In 1864? Can you actually believe that? It's almost unbelievable, but it happened. But in the context of a novel that would have to be made believable. Indeed it isn't enough for the writer to say, 'but it really happened.' The writer has to make the event seem believable in the story. On pages 28 and 29 of the paperback of *How Not to Write a Novel*, there is an excellent passage: too long to quote in full here without invoking copyright problems, entitled 'Why Your Job is Harder than God's'. It's very much worth reading.

19. Language and words

Let's now look at the mechanics of language, which after all is the tool writers use.

We are limited as writers by the fact that we can't create life. This is true of all artists. Sculptors use inanimate and durable materials to create a physical object that evokes a living being or an inanimate entity, but is neither. Michelangelo's *La Pieta* is a great masterpiece but, ultimately, it's not the same as a living, breathing woman and her baby. Only a deity (if you believe in one) or the life force, can create actual life. As writers we are doubly handicapped if you think about it. We can't create life from the tools we use, as the tools we use are words, which by definition are merely linguistic tools for evoking something, just as an artist uses oil paints or a sculptor uses plaster of Paris or marble.

Language is a spontaneous prehistoric invention which probably evolved in tandem with the evolution of our species. Very likely early forms of humans had some sort of language and as human beings developed, language got more sophisticated. *Homo sapiens* has been around for 100,000 years or maybe more than that. The languages that were spoken 50,000 years ago were no less sophisticated than they are today.

We have a larger number of technical terms in our languages today, but people in the past still had highly sophisticated languages. Very possibly earlier forms of language spoken by earlier forms of mankind were less sophisticated than the languages spoken by *homo sapiens*, but there is no evidence at all that there are any 'primitive' languages spoken by *homo sapiens*.

Writing is fantastically more recent a development and invention than language. Writing was invented seven or eight thousand years BC, so it is at the most about 10,000 years old. There is evidence that writing first came about, as you might expect, as a way of people remembering who owned what in more complex societies. It's no coincidence that writing evolved about the same time as people tended to move away from rural, Neolithic settings, and live in more sophisticated urban communities.

By the way, writing is a form of setting down *language*, not thought. You can't set down human experience directly, you have to set things down in language. One reason the hieroglyphs in Ancient Egypt were extremely difficult to decipher was because the people seeking to decipher them initially thought hieroglyphs all depicted the things they were pictures of. As it happens, some did, but most were phonetic symbols of the Ancient Egyptian language, which by the time people in the eighteenth century tried to decipher it, was a dead language. However, some people who tried to decipher the hieroglyphs fortunately knew that the still surviving church language Coptic was related to the Ancient Egyptian language. This made things a lot easier for them and eventually facilatated decipherment.

So words are limited tools. They're not inherently all that potent. The word 'beautiful' is nowhere near as potent as seeing beauty.

So what's the upside of words? Why are words potentially so powerful for a writer? One upside is that words give us access to experience that we wouldn't necessarily want to take part in ourselves. We might read a thriller such as *The Day of the Jackal* about people getting killed. We most likely don't really want to be in a situation in our lives where we might be killed at any moment, so words give us the opportunity to experience vicarious excitement, in the same way that the screen-based entertainment does the same visually.

Also, words are durable. Once words are set down they will transcend the end of our lives. If you and I write a novel that is good enough it will be read by people after we are dead.

But words are only immortal if we use them well, and this brings us on to the particular way that words should be used in novels.

20. Show and tell

Many writers who are starting out to write fiction read about 'show' and 'tell' and get worried and stressed about what these terms really mean in a practical sense for fiction-writers.

But in fact there's no need to get worried or stressed about these two terms, although I would certainly agree that they are not only essential to understand but in many ways understanding them is at the very heart of what fiction-writing is all about.

Very often literary agents and people teaching creative writing tell you that you should use 'show' rather than 'tell'. This is actually inaccurate. What is more accurate is to say that *you should use 'show' when it needs to be used and you should use 'tell' when it needs to be used.*

One metaphor I find quite useful when coaching fiction writers is to ask them to see themselves a boxer. A boxer will have a right and a left hand and of course which hand is the strongest will depend on whether the boxer is right-handed or left-handed. I'm not going to say that a boxer's right hand will be his or her 'show' hand and his left hand the 'tell'; all I will say is that yes, generally when you write fiction you should use 'show' rather than 'tell', in other words you should use the hand which is most appropriate for the particular moment of the boxing match. But certainly you should see yourself as a writing machine who as a boxing machine has two hands to fight with.

All right, so when should you use 'show' and when should you use 'tell'? In order to arrive at a useful answer to this vital question I'd like to ask you to consider what the nature of using words to tell a story really is in the first place.

People who are literate, which most of us are nowadays, tend to think that somehow writing is a more fundamental and primary form of language than spoken language, but this is not the case. All languages, without exception, were spoken before they were written down. It's not known exactly when human language evolved but the strong likelihood is that language evolved with the evolution of humanity and that earlier forms of our species had their own language though perhaps not as complex nor as subtle as human language.

There is, by the way, no such thing as a 'primitive language': whether a language is spoken by a tribe with a rudimentary technology on some far off island or by people of a modern urban society, the language is equally complex and subtle. As the famous linguist Edward Sapir once remarked in his book *Language* (1921): *When it comes to linguistic form, Plato walked with the Macedonian swineherd, Confucius with the head-hunting savage of Assam.*

In other words all languages of *homo sapiens* are equally complex and indeed many that are spoken today are still not written down, including, by the way, most modern dialects of English, that only exist in a standardised written form in the standard spelling of modern English.

I make these points to emphasise that language is inherently an artificial construct. Literate people tend to think of language as written words flowing out of someone's mouth, but in fact English could be written perfectly adequately in all sorts of different alphabets that aren't used and indeed it could also be written in Chinese characters if we felt motivated to do so, although it is true that Chinese characters tend to be a more satisfactory way of writing down a language, such as Chinese itself, which is highly analytical in how it breaks down meaning into single units.

It's true that people sometimes write novels entirely in the present tense, which I don't really think works although certainly having isolated passages written in the present tense can make them more vivid. The problem with a novel written purely in the present tense is that one wonders how exactly the writer has written it if he's carrying out the experience as he's writing. Does he have a notepad with him to record things as they are spontaneously happening?

As words are by definition at a remove from the lived experience, it follows as a matter of common sense that if you want to evoke a lived experience you need to use words very carefully.

Many writers who are starting out write what they think are novels but which are in fact simply summaries of action. For example:

Jackie was a very attractive woman.

or here is another example:

John and Helen made love that afternoon and really enjoyed themselves.

These two sentences are highly typical of the kind of thing I see in novels, or rather samples of novels that are sent to me at Canterbury Literary Agency.

Why do I think that such writing doesn't work? You may argue that it does convey meaning. I'm not denying this; it does and you may also argue that the grammar and syntax are correct, which they are. But this is not real fiction-writing. It doesn't work because it's just a *summary* of life rather than anything that actually *evokes* life. A written summary of life is 'tell'; a written evocation of life is 'show'.

For example, let's look at the sentence 'Jackie was a very attractive woman.'

It doesn't actually tell us anything real about Jackie whatsoever. One major problem is that it doesn't give any specific terms on which any assessment of her attraction or otherwise can be based. For example, if someone only finds plump women attractive and somebody else only finds thin women attractive then both will think of Jackie, when she is described as attractive, as attractive in their own way. There isn't any objective standard which could evoke her attraction. It's just a 'tell' sentence and as something belonging in a novel it is by and large completely useless.

But it isn't difficult to make it more effective. You could simply give us some more information about what makes Jackie attractive. For example: *Jackie had long golden hair like pirate treasure, an impish grin, a pert little nose and green eyes which when you looked at them seemed to suggest a wealth of exciting possibilities.*

I not suggesting this is brilliant writing but it does illustrate you can do a lot better than just describing her as 'attractive'. What you need to do, when you want to bring Jackie's attractiveness alive, is *give the reader sensory information from the real world* which will in effect allow you to *report, in a way that evokes life,* what Jackie is like.

Similarly, the sentence about John and Helen making love is hopeless for a piece of fiction because it doesn't give the reader anything. When authors write this kind of amateurish stuff I always say to them, 'Why don't you give the reader more information so that they can enjoy the scene too?' I've already explained how you need to give the sensory information which will allow the scene to be evoked in your readers' imagination. I suggest that you don't describe the scene from an authorial point of view but from the perspective of one of the characters and get into their heads and invoke the love-making in terms of what it means sensuously to the viewpoint character. For example:

John never forgot that afternoon with Helen. Even now, years later, he remembered how red her lips were, how white her teeth and how kissing her deeply and long had made him feel he was entering a new world that he'd hardly ever guessed could exist.

I'm not suggesting that's brilliant but you surely by now get the hang of what I'm doing here: which is basically converting a piece of writing that is just words, i.e. 'tell' into 'show'.

It really isn't very difficult. Anthony Burgess, a great novelist, once remarked that a good novel was basically made up of sense data and I would agree with that. You see, we are physical beings living in a real world, we're not brains in goldfish tanks. We are physical beings who will bleed if we're cut, who will one day die, who need to eat and drink and to appease other bodily functions. That's what makes us human. It follows that if we are writing about other human beings we need to evoke them in just the same way. You should also realise by now that some adjectives - 'attractive' is a good example - are pretty much useless for fiction-writing anyway because they are so abstract and we need to be specific in fiction-writing. *In fiction-writing particularisation is the name of the game.* Calling someone attractive may be OK if you're discussing somebody with your friends over a few pints; there's nothing wrong with using that word in that context if you want to. But if you want to be a novelist you need to use words that are much more evocative and give your readers the sense of somebody existing, and things happening in the real world.

So that is basically what 'show' is: giving the reader

real sensory data from the real world. And as we are such a highly visual species, visual sensory data is especially important, though sounds, smells, touch and taste matter very much too:

When Edward ran into the kitchen the hiss and smell of the steak and onions frying in butter on the hob made him feel giddy with hunger.

In novels, the most usual sounds are dialogue and here please bear in mind a fundamental point about 'show' which is this: *all dialogue is by definition 'show'.*

This doesn't mean that all dialogue is necessarily good dialogue but because dialogue exactly mirrors the event - the speech in the real world - all dialogue is 'show', which is why Shakespeare's plays are all 'show', apart from the stage directions.

So, am I therefore saying that there's no need for 'tell' in a novel at all?

No, I'm certainly not saying that and do beware of creative writing teachers who imply that 'tell' is a sort of inferior cousin of 'show'. In fact, as I've said, that's not the case. 'Tell' is just a *different* way of telling a story and, as I say, you need it in your boxing armoury as much as 'show'.

So when do you use 'tell'? The answer is, as I imagine you'll have gathered by now, that you use tell when you want to summarise certain events in order to move the story on briskly.

As a novelist you have to select the events to relate that will best develop your story and will push your story forward. Very often characters in novels do things that don't need to be explained to the reader in detail. For example, if your characters are flying to the United States it may not be necessary for you to say anything about the flight other than, for example, 'John and Helen arrived in New York early that evening and went to their hotel room and straight to bed.' That may be all you need. But if for example Jon and Helen have a momentous conversation or the flight is hijacked or something else of dramatic importance within the novel takes place, then of course you need to chronicle it as 'show' which means you give the dialogue, and bring the scene alive by reporting sense data to the reader that will let them visualise and immerse themselves in the scene. And also, by the way, if you have already established the nature of the particular experience in preceding excellent 'show' material, there may not be any need to repeat it. If we already know that John and Helen have a great time in bed there are only so many times the reader wants to know about this.

A good tip if you are depicting a scene which is really too long to relate in its entirety is to give the reader a taste of it by using 'show' at the start and then 'tell' to summarise what happened the rest of the time. For example, if John and Helen are having a romantic dinner in a Manhattan restaurant, you can perhaps give the reader a couple of pages of passionate, excited, romantic dialogue and then summarise the rest of the meal in 'tell' and your reader won't feel cheated.

After all, if a novel was only written in 'show' it would be longer than the Bible.

But again, let's remember that while 'show' cannot be said to be superior to 'tell', 'show' is a much more useful device than 'tell' for bringing your story to life. And that is what really matters, because ideally a novel *should read like life on the page*.

My ultimate advice would be for you to conceive of your novel as a kind of movie written down in words. That way you won't be in danger of doing silly lifeless summaries that tell of events that you really need to be evoking. I can't tell you which events to evoke but the answer is that it should be the dramatically significant ones.

Incidentally, as I'm writing about 'show' here, this is perhaps a good place for me to make some suggestions about how you write about sex.

In the past novels tended to avoid specific sexual scenes and in the nineteenth century writers had the excuse that the middle-classes in most European countries and in the United States would not tolerate explicit descriptions of sexuality in fiction. In fact Dickens was very conscious of this restriction, often complaining to his friends about it. He fathered at least nine children himself so we can be fairly confident that he knew about sex.

All that said, you can't write about sex in an anatomical hard-core way if you want to get published by a mainstream publisher because most readers don't like it and besides sex is exciting because of the emotional resonance between the characters not because of the anatomical things they are doing to each other. In fact, writing about sex anatomically is a complete turn-off to the reader and rapidly becomes unreadable. Instead, don't refrain from giving some good 'show' physical details but don't lay on everything with a trowel either. Think of your own sexual experiences and how what matters is a particular look in the eyes of your lover or a particular curve of their shoulders or something that is not hard-core at all but actually triggers emotions in you. Here, for example, is a beautiful piece of writing about love-making from Ben Parker's remarkable novel *Beetlebrow the Thief* (2018). Beetlebrow and Pook are two young vagabond women who have met each other and gradually fallen in love while carrying out a complex and dangerous mission in the hostile and generally highly creepy society in which they found themselves living. Beetlebrow and Pook have just finished their supper of porridge around a campfire.

Beetlebrow looked at Pook's face. She saw the purple rings under her eyes, and a dab of porridge to the right of her mouth. She reached out her left hand towards Pook's face and wiped the porridge away with her thumb. Pook's smile rose. Beetlebrow glanced at the tall man. His pin-prick eyes were staring at the flames.

Within an hour the fire was becoming low. Beetlebrow felt her eyes drawing closed.

She noticed the tall man lying asleep on the ground beside the embers. She glanced at Pook. The right side of

Pook's face was shadowed while its left was lit by the faint orange glow from the remains of the fire.

Beetlebrow felt Pook's hand touching her waist, and her soft fingers drifting across her skin. She heard the branches crackling.

Beetlebrow's throat was dry and her lips were chapped. She leant towards Pook. She saw Pook's brown eyes become lit with flames as their mouths drew together.

I think you'd be hard pushed to find a passage about the initiation of gentle love-making that's more effective than that. In fact, I've been working with Ben for some years and the first draft of *Beetlebrow and the Thief* features a great deal of authorial intervention from Ben and our work together was substantially about liberating his talent by making Beetlebrow in most scenes the character viewpoint and having events happening from her perspective. Notice how that scene when she starts to make love with Pook is far more effective from Beetlebrow's point of view than if an author were intruding into the scene and pulling the strings. When I meet a writer who is married and am coaching them about reducing or indeed eliminating the amount of authorial intervention in their novels, I often ask them how they would feel, when they are in bed with their spouse, if an author was in the room describing their intimate activities to readers. I once asked this question of a professional lady I was coaching and she seemed quite taken aback by my suggestion, which was the idea because of course in real life there aren't any authors to comment on the action and that's why I don't think there should be any in novels.

The influence of movies has made readers more demanding (though possibly unconsciously) of the 'show' in a novel. After all, movies are all show, except those occasional parts at the start of movies set in classical times (including *Gladiator*), where you get a bit of prose on the screen at the start which sets the scene, and then you go into the movie. The bit of prose at the start itself shows that movies are an art-form whose narrative form developed from prose fiction and prose histories.

When you recall a novel you have enjoyed, it's the show passages you mainly remember. And yes, the reason is because we are physical beings in a physical world, and we're engaged by physical events. Which of us would rather read a letter from the person we love rather than spend an evening with them?

There are 'tell-words', too. These are usually abstract words whose meaning is imprecise. Certainly you have to understand as a novelist that using a word like 'beautiful', for example, is an inadequate way of describing the character. Why?

Let's think again of a beautiful female character. If we let the reader see her beauty (e.g. her glossy, very straight shoulder-length black hair; her pale, fine-grained, creamy skin, her bright blue eyes, her even, white teeth and her rather full lips emphasised with just a touch of light, orange-red lipstick) that's fine. But if you just say she's 'beautiful'and leave it at that, it doesn't work at all. Why not? Because you're a communicator and your reader does not have the same terms of reference as you do.

If, say, your reader comes from a very different culture to you, they may think of beauty in a woman in a different way to how you do.

Or if you're writing a science fiction novel and you say 'Zyx was beautiful' and Zyx is actually a female pterodactyl-type dragon, on her planet being beautiful might mean having very shiny green horns. That's fine, as long as we know what the cultural references are. If we have established that that's the rule in Zyx's culture, 'Zyx flapped her wings and stood up to her greatest extent. Her green horns glistened. They shone like the star that ruled her galaxy. Myz was transfixed. He'd never seen such beauty.' You need to particularise what you mean by beauty. And that, that particularisation, is indeed the essence of what literary art is.

So if you just say 'Zyx was beautiful', you are not really saying very much because there is no practical, essentially visible, standard to which the word 'beautiful' relates. I'm not gay, but if I were, I would doubtless see beauty in a different way than a heterosexual man would see beauty. If I only find black women attractive I would admire a different kind of physical female beauty than if I only found Scandinavian women attractive. If you haven't established the terms of reference then your readers will, by default, use the terms of reference that they're familiar with. That's the reason why you can't just use the word 'beautiful' and expect your reader to know what you mean. Besides, you want your story to live, so why not give the reader some really great sense data? And that is why good novels tend to be comprised of nouns and fairly concrete adjectives.

You can say, for example, 'golden hair'. That makes sense. 'She blushed a fine crimson.' We know what that looks like. But you should avoid abstract words like 'beautiful' or 'wonderful' in the narrative voice. It's different, though, if a character uses them. Maybe you have a character, Teresa, in a novel you're writing, and in that character's world everybody is wonderful. Teresa might think someone wonderful just because they live in Tunbridge Wells. Or Teresa might think someone wonderful for having two cars, and soon we realise that Teresa describing someone as wonderful says more about Teresa than about anyone else. Suddenly, you have done what a novelist must do and set a particular use of a word in context with a character's personality. You have used the very fact that Teresa uses the abstract noun so willingly. You've used that as a way of finding her as a character. It works very well. That's the point you see. And this is why mastering the tools of writing fiction is so important: you can use them as a way of making your story live and enthrall yor readers.

21. Suspense

No novel will be interesting unless it contains suspense. Suspense basically means delaying revelation. A good novel does this, I think, at two levels: firstly, in the major elements of the plot and the delayed revelations that draw you to want to read to the end: secondly, in the incidents that populate the story and which reach individual conclusions at the end of a particular chapter or section or even at the end of a couple of pages.

In making your novel full of suspense, you are mirroring life, which is itself rich with suspense. Do you know every detail of what is going to be happening in your life tomorrow? No, you don't. You don't even definitely know whether you're going to be alive in twenty-four hours' time.

Will John propose to Betty? Is the tumour benign or malevolent? Will the solo free climber stay on the side of the mountain or fall off? Is Debbie pregnant? Can the asteroid be prevented from hitting the planet Earth? Will the bomb defuser manage to make the bomb safe without being blown to pieces?

These are just some of many examples of a myriad potential suspenseful situations. Your novel needs plenty of such situations, both within individual chapters and as part of the main story of your book.

Ken Follett, interviewed in the Christmas 1993 edition of the US journal *Writing Magazine* by Judith Spelman, said something I thought particularly interesting when Judith asked him what the secret was of writing page-turning material. He replied:

'It is a pattern, you see, composed of small dramas within a large drama. You must make sure that before one small drama is resolved, another has begun. When you are reading you think *I'll just find out what happens at the end of this scene.* But before you get to the end of the scene, your curiosity is caught by a development that is going to create the drama in the following scene. Then you think you will read the next scene...'

That is very nicely expressed by Mr Follett, and I strongly suggest you follow his advice.

22. The need for your story to be logical

A fundamental requirement is that your story needs to be logical, which means that the motivations and behaviour of characters need to make sense.

This is not always easy to be sure about when you are writing. There are often grey areas about what will seem logical and plausible in terms of motivation and behaviour.

For example, I've always felt that the scene in *Titanic* where Rose - desperate to find Jack and knowing he is being held below deck after being placed under arrest, encounters Thomas Andrews the shipmaker (brilliantly played by Victor Garber) and Andrews tells her where to find Jack - doesn't work. The way Andrews has been drawn, by this point in the movie I think we believe he would help Rose and take her down to find Jack, but if he did then Rose's predicament would be less difficult and less dramatic. This is only a small glitch in a splendid movie, but it does show how there comes a point when you have to accept that your characters will in effect take over the story and do with it what they want to do with it. They will often tell you themselves whether what you are writing about them is believable.

This said, of course you may not agree with what I said just now about Thomas Andrew. We all have somewhat different takes on what we're prepared to accept as believable; there is no objective standard of believability, there are just opinions and the writer has to anticipate what the consensus might be.

After all, we respond to events emotionally in different ways. One man might respond to being dumped by the same lady to shrugging it off and dating another the following night; another man might respond - illegally - by devoting the next five years of his life to stalking her. I myself tend to respond to being dumped by writing a novel about the lady which casts her in a positive light.

What matters, of course, is how logical the motivation and behaviour seems in terms of the character, but that is not always easy to be sure about. A good mentor, adviser and editor can be crucially important to you here as in all other areas of your novel-writing.

23. Editing and improving your novel

Which brings me to this vital point: no novel worth reading is ever ready for sending to the publisher the moment it is finished. Your book will ALWAYS need more work, and that means that you need to edit your novel mercilessly.

Will: *'editing is gruelling but neccessary. Books are never finished only abandoned.'*

Above all, let at least some time elapse between finishing you novel, and revising it. In fact, I also advise you to use the services of a professional editor before you let a literary agent or publisher see it. You will probably simply need to invest in doing this. Most literary agents are not editors; if the book is not almost already as good as it can be (which most likely the book won't be) they most likely won't take it on. I'm an exception; as a writer myself I do give editorial advice, but only if I like the book, or the part I've seen.

There will very likely be a limit to how polished you can make your book without some professional help. In today's cut-throat publishing world, few agents or publishers can afford to help a writer polish a promising novel into a publishable novel unless the writer already has a name and is making them money, and that still doesn't solve the problem of how the writer gets his first book good enough to be successful. So, seek professional editorial advice, and above all be prepared to listen to advice about making cuts, and to converting 'tell' to 'show'.

24. Summing up

Think of your camp-fire story-teller trying to earn his or her supper of roasted sausages (or roasted peppers if he or she is vegetarian) and it's all clear. We want a hero or heroine. We want a beginning that is interesting. We want a story that is full of significant events without unnecessary digressions. We want everything significant to be pursued or else don't bother mentioning it to start with.

We want the story to be told in spare, compelling, concise language where every word is there for a purpose and does its work well. In the past, language was no less potentially powerful and evocative than it is today. It's a fair bet that ten thousand or maybe even fifty thousand years ago there was once a time when a camp-fire tale-teller said, 'She was beautiful,' and a member of the audience said, 'What on earth is that supposed to mean?' The camp-fire narrator would not be given his delicious campfire-roasted sausages until he'd provided 'show' details about what he meant by her beauty, otherwise he hadn't done his job properly. And no writer is going to get his or her sausage, so to speak, until he or she has done his or her job well, too.

If I make you a chair with only three legs, you'd think, 'This chair's rubbishy' and you'll ask me to put a fourth leg on it, at least unless it's a three-legged stool. But if I make you a chair with five or six or seven legs on it, you will ask me to chop off all the extra legs above four. You don't need them. So all we're doing as novelists is doing exactly what the camp-fire narrator does, or what a chair-maker needs to do.

How Not to Write a Novel is a useful and entertaining book and I would recommend you read it. However, there is a serious downside to it: the book makes the whole job of writing a novel more daunting than it needs to be and less fun and enjoyable than it can be. *How Not to Write a Novel* tells you what not to do, it makes you feel there's lots of pitfalls, which indeed there are, but if you have a great story and great characters, you will have a lot of fun writing your story, and lots of the work will be done by your characters, as after a while your characters will indeed tell the story for you.

Remember: the *author* is the *author*ity. You are the authority and responsible for making your novel great.

Ernest Hemingway said that as a writer he tried to produce what he called the 'one true sentence'. He meant a very straightforward sentence the reader would accept.

Ken Follett, on his website, says that he wants to write the sentence that the reader thinks they could write for themselves.

As a writer myself, I'd like to think that I could produce sentences the reader *wouldn't* have thought of. But all the same, funnily enough, and this is something I learned fairly recently in writing fiction, a lot of the stuff in good novels is fairly everyday material. That's a fair point to make, actually. A character in a novel can't have absolutely amazing things happening all the time, or be doing amazing things all the time or he or she would lose credibility. The scenes should be interesting but you are going to have to have some straightforward scenes too, because if you're too outlandish you lose your reader. Even movie stuntmen need time off in their trailers to have a snooze and a coffee. As for great Victorian novels - *David Copperfield* for example - much of the material they contain is actually rather mundane but told in a wonderful way.

Even *The Lord of the Rings* is ultimately just about people in Middle Earth going about their business. Yes, they've got strange names and it's a different kind of world with different races, but ultimately *The Lord of the Rings* (1954) - I'm not saying it's ordinary, it's obviously a very fine piece of work - is set in a recognisable real world. It's not crazy. And crucially, the motivation of Sauron and Sauraman and the bad guys, they're recognisable motivations. Sauron is trying to take over the world. The good guys are trying to protect what they regard as infinitely valuable, like the Shire with its hobbits and the strawberries and cream and the grass and the love-making and the smoking, the holidays and the meals.

Sauron is not trying to do something bizarre and mad, like trying to make everyone wear their underpants outside their trousers. His motivations are emotionally easily recognisable. I think we have to tread delicate balances as novelists between what is familiar and what is unfamiliar.

Yes, we have to make things exciting, we have to use riveting words that make our books exciting and interesting, but we have to write a story in a recognisable real world. I think that's a very important point to make. In the Harry Potter world the goodies and baddies alike actually behave very logically.

The real world we live in is pretty haphazard in its allocation of destinies, and things happening in it can seem pretty random. Things happen in the world that can hurt us no matter how nice and kind we are, or think we are. The agenda of other people is often very different from ours. So, yes, the world is full of potential disappointments and upsets, and the fact that those disappointments and upsets are usually fairly random doesn't make them any less disappointing or upsetting. But as writers, we write stories that can make the world make sense to us, which is why, when you are writing, ultimately the words you produce are very dear to your heart, and if you make them work then you will find yourself being rewarded for that with status and money, and something even more important: great self-respect and self-esteem.

I think writing fiction - or, more to the point, writing fiction that is going well - is the most exhilarating job in the world. When it goes well, even without great recognition from the outside world, it is a compensating force for all the things in life that can disappoint: people, relationships, the practical difficulties of life, one's health, and one's career, those things can be very disappointing, even for people who on the face of things seem quite successful.

Ken Follett once described his profession of novelist as 'organising daydreams' which of course it is to a large extent, but I think it's much more than that. Writing a novel can put you in touch with the truth of the human condition in a way that is more exciting than almost anything else in life. I think the only thing that is more exciting is truly passionate love.

Writing fiction - and reading great fiction - provides a shield against all of life's disappointments, not least the biggest disappointment of all: that at some point we grow old and frail and die. But our written words, if forked with flame and power and passion, may outdistance death and conquer it, just as love does.

So let's get to work.

Appendix 1:

Specific guidance about mistakes I often find in submissions made to Canterbury Literary Agency

If you want to be a surgeon you need to learn what a scalpel is and if you want to be an airline pilot you need to know what an engine is. Many people who aspire to write fiction can't be bothered to master basic elements of punctuation and other essential elements of writing prose. I don't think there's any point in me being too kind about people who make the mistakes I'm going to list in this appendix, because it's not in their interests that I am kind about this. You simply need to accept that writing prose, whether fiction or anything else, is an art as well as a science and the scientific elements are matters that are either objectively right or wrong and you need to get them right. Writing prose fiction is difficult enough without making unnecessary mistakes and so, here, in no particular order, are problems I find over and over again when I see submissions to Canterbury Literary Agency.

1. *Its* or *It's*

    This is one of the most fundamental things you need to get right if you're serious about being a writer.

Its is a possessive form of *it*.

For example, *The dog has hurt its foot.*

A common mistake is that *it's* which is simply a shortened form of *it is* is used instead of *its*. For some reason the mistake is almost always this way round rather than the other way round. For example, you find a sentence like: *The train will arrive in it's own good time.*

I'm not going to say much about this. You simply need to get it right or stop trying to be a writer. You need to check all uses of *its* and *it's* in your work before you send it off to any professional.

2. *Your* and *You're*

   Again, this is a common mistake even among educated people. Very simply, *your* is the possessive form of *you* while *you're* is a shorter form of *you are*.

3. *There* and *Their*

   There indicates a location, whereas *their* is the possessive form of *they*.

4. Here's a particularly annoying mistake that is horribly common. Writers sometimes give the impression they think that 'said John' for example is a sentence in itself, but it never is. You get something like this:

   'I'm coming home tonight.' Said John.

   In fact it should be:

   'I'm coming home tonight,' said John.

People make this mistake because they somehow imagine that a verb indicating who says something such as, *'said,' 'replied,' 'asked,'* can be a main verb and it can't. If you're using a speech-indicating verb the sentence doesn't finish till the end of the actual sentence which must include the speech-indicating verb.

You don't necessarily need to use speech-indicating verbs although if you've got more than two people talking in the scene I recommend you use it fairly often so that the reader knows who is saying what.

5. Using commas

    The use of commas in novels by inexperienced writers is often very poor. The rule is really very simple, you should use a comma when you would take a breath if you were reading it out. By the way, always make sure you put a comma in after dialogue and before a speech indicator. For example, a common mistake I encounter is *'Let's go home' said John.*

    Clearly, you need a comma before the quote mark and by the way the comma should always come before the quote mark in normal dialogue.

6. Another common mistake when using commas is that writers don't bother putting a comma before the name of someone who is addressed in some dialogue. For example, *'Shall we go to the cafe Claudius?'*

    If you write like this the reader may well wonder whether the cafe is called Claudius. In fact, if you were addressing Claudius you would take a breath before doing so, so make sure you put a comma in pretty much every case where someone is addressing a thing or an object and you are using their name.

The following passage, posted on Facebook by my friend the New York literary agent Russell Galen, to whom this book is dedicated, speaks for itself.

I have an obsession when reading unpublished manuscripts: incorrect use of the vocative case.

This refers to a sentence in which a person is being addressed. The name needs to be separated from the rest of the sentence by a comma.

For instance: 'Please take the dog for a walk, John.' not 'Please take the dog for a walk John.'

I don't expect writers to know every rule of grammar. I forgive (and commit) many other errors. But if you get this wrong, you have a tin ear for dialogue. That's a symptom which is always accompanied by some deep, fatal disease so for me it's grounds for rejection.

Had to get that off my chest! It drives me crazy.

Russ might have also added, to use another dog-related example, that in many cases incorrect punctuation of the vocative creates terrible ambiguities. For example, 'Please tell me about your dog John' could mean the dog was called John if you don't put a comma after the word 'dog'.

7. Make sure you let the reader know where a location is and what it looks like when you first introduce it.

If there's any danger that the reader will not know where the particular location is you should do them the courtesy of explaining that before you move on with the story. If your book's set in London and New York the reader can reasonably be expected to know where those places are but if it's set in, for example, the town of Pori in Finland where I used to live when I taught English in that excellent country many years ago, you should give the reader the courtesy of explaining where Pori actually is.

Similarly, make sure you give character descriptions when you first introduce the character so that the reader can enjoy thinking about what the character looks like and can enjoy encountering them. Don't do what many inexperienced writers do which is mention a new character's name and then four or five pages later on give the description of the character. After all, if you're at a dinner party and met someone at seven o'clock at the dinner party you can see what they look like immediately; you don't need to wait until half past seven or eight o'clock to see that.

When you're writing a first-person novel, it's perfectly legitimate for you to introduce a character to the reader through the sensibility of the narrator and that might mean that the first time the narrator sees the new character he or she doesn't fully assimilate the appearance of the character or only does so briefly. In *The Mating Game,* a first-person novel by myself and Jovanka Houska, the very first time Vanny, who is visiting her father Godfrey (who prefers to be called God) in Monte Carlo sees the French-Portuguese woman Helene with whom Vanny is destined to have an affair, she notices Helene briefly.

The tea was brought to us by an extremely pretty, reserved-looking waitress, with tanned skin and beautiful long glossy black hair that was frankly quite a bit like mine. Dad thanked her courteously and obviously very sincerely, added a tip when he signed the bill, and I watched with admiration as she expertly dealt with his flirty comments.

That is the first time Vanny actually sees Helene but she only fully assimilates Helene that evening when Helene brings her a cup of tea to her room.

I was still crying when a knock came on the bedroom door. I wiped my eyes quickly and got off the bed, made my way clumsily over to the door and opened it.

The woman standing there was a beautiful woman, with tanned skin and long black hair, who I recognised immediately as the waitress who had served Dad and me earlier that day in the hotel cafe. I let her in, keeping my eyes down so she wouldn't see the state of my face.

'Your tea, madam,' said the woman as she came in, carrying in a silver-gilt tray with tea things on it.

'Thanks,' I mumbled. 'Can you - could you just put it on the table, please?'

'Yes, of course,' she said, and she laid the tray down on a low, glass-topped table in the middle of the room.

*Once she had, she glanced at me, and of course she
saw I was in tears.*

*'Is everything all right, madam?' she asked, softly
and gently.*

*I tossed back my tears. 'Please, don't call me that. I'm
not married and I very much doubt I ever will be.'*

That is the start of the scene in which Vanny and
Helene make love.

8. Make any manuscript you submit as professional as
possible. The simple fact is that too many aspiring
first-time novelists don't take enough trouble over their
work. In many ways I do sympathise: by definition,
first-time novelists are unlikely to be earning any money
from writing their first novel, and writing a novel will
take ages and is extremely hard work and very likely
they do another job to pay the bills while they're writing
it in the evenings or at weekends. I know the temptation
is to get the novel off to a professional sooner rather
than later because you're desperate to find out if your
own perception of it as pretty good is actually justified.
But in my opinion I would simply insist to yourself that
you don't send any work of fiction or non-fiction to any
professional till at least a week has elapsed before you've
finished it and you've given it another extra polish. Oh,
and by the way, when you send a novel to a literary
agent please don't say in the email that your friends
or any relatives like it because that's irrelevant, as I've
already said, and above all please don't say, 'I hope you

like it' because that always seems to me to be rather like a veiled threat.

Do take the trouble to find out if the literary agency you are approaching actually does handle the kind of book you've written because otherwise you're just wasting your time. Many literary agents specialise in certain genres of books and you should try and find out which one is the right one. In the UK, if you're courteous, you can normally find a lot out on the telephone or using the internet but in the United States publishers and indeed agents arrange things and it is virtually impossible to get any information on the phone and in fact receptionists are briefed not to give email addresses out.

One important tip is that you can join a really brilliant US-based website called Publishers' Marketplace which costs $25 a month to subscribe to but you don't need to subscribe for more than a month if you don't want to and that gives you access and all sorts of useful ways of searching for names and email addresses of anyone who is of any importance in the US publishing industry. I used to despair of ever getting good contacts in the United States but I have subscribed to Publishers' Marketplace now for a couple of years and it's absolutely a godsend.

Finally, take care over your submission email. In most places you will be submitting to an agent rather than a publisher because most publishers don't take unagencied submissions nowadays. Try to keep your email succinct, to the point and professional. If you are the kind of person who is a little bit mentally unbalanced, which many writers are, do at least try your best not to show it in the first email you send to a prospective agent. Focus on what you've written, how long the book is, what the market is and if there's any reason why you are the right person to write it.

9. Clichés

Clichés are phrases, often similes but by no means always, that have become hackneyed through over-use. There's no room for compromise here: if you want to be taken seriously as a writer of any description, but especially if you are writing fiction or narrative non-fiction, you simply can't use clichés in your work or you'll look stupid. And I mean stupid. Clichés bring down the opinion of anyone reading your work because they will think, perfectly justifiably, that you care so little about your readers that you can't even be bothered to think of a phrase or expression which you've not already seen in print.

If you want to find out whether something you thought of saying in your novel is a cliché or not, there are plenty of websites which list clichés. There's really no need to spend your time doing that, though, simply follow the golden rule that you should not use a phrase, especially a simile, which you have already seen in print. If you have a character who says to her husband, for example, 'You look like you've just seen a ghost,' that is a terrible cliché and in fact it's more likely that what the husband has actually seen is not so much a ghost but a spectre of the departing potential career of the would-be novelist. The only time a cliché is justified is if you have a character in your novel who is annoying because he or she keeps speaking in clichés. But then you need to make very clear that the idea is that the character is like that. Don't use that characterisation as an excuse to fill dialogue with excessive numbers of clichés or even your reader, tolerant to some extent of the character because of the way you've portrayed him or her, will get annoyed.

We don't spend our money on novels to find phrases in them which we could have written ourselves, what's the point in doing that? No, follow the golden rule of avoiding clichés and you'll be fine. A good technique for avoiding clichés is simply to invent your own such as by playing around with a cliché and making it more interesting. So if you have a character who would - if you were using a cliché - indeed say to her husband, 'you look like you've just seen a ghost' you could avoid this being a cliché by playing around with the phrase and saying, for example, 'You look like you've just seen the ghost of great-uncle Fred.' That works well because it is a tacit nod to the recognition that the phrase is a cliché but the creation of a new way of presenting the cliché makes the expression fresh and readable.

10. Speech indicators

Speech indicators are phrases or, sometimes, sentences which, as the name suggests, indicate which character in your book has said something. There's quite a lot to say about speech indicators but I'll try and keep this concise.

The first thing to say is that if there are only two characters in the scene you can often dispense with speech indicators completely although you do need to remind the reader from time to time who is saying what, otherwise the poor reader will have to go back to the top of the page and mentally work out who spoke the latest piece of dialogue. I once read a novel by a well-known novelist of considerable talent who continually in his novel failed to do this and it was extremely irritating to have to keep looking further up the dialogue to work out who was saying what. My advice would be that if you have a scene with only two people in it, remind the reader about every three or four lines who is saying what.

Oh, don't make the fundamental beginner's mistake of always including the name of the person being spoken to when someone speaks. I have already mentioned that you need to put a comma before the name of the person who is being addressed if you use the name in dialogue but there is often no need to use the name at all.

You often get this mistake in screenplays of otherwise perfectly good movies where the unfortunate actors have lines where they are continually saying the name of the person they are addressing which in real life we don't normally do unless we want to make a point.

For example:

'I don't know why you keep asking Mary out, John, she's much too good for you!'

In that kind of sentence we would put in the name of the person we are speaking to but normally we don't but certainly you mustn't do it as a routine. I notice that when I'm writing the first draft of a novel I do sometimes do this and then spend time editing these names out, but it would be better if I didn't do it in the first place.

Now let's move on to the question of what actual verb you use in the speech indicator.

Well, obviously the most familiar verb to use would be 'said,' 'replied,' 'asked' and 'returned.' Dickens, by the way, is a great fan of 'returned' and employs it often. However, he also uses 'said' a great deal as well. Because writers know that repeating words in the same sentence or same paragraph is often bad stylistically, they tend to think the same rule applies to the word 'said.' Curiously enough, it doesn't; whereas if you were to use the same phrase several times in the paragraph that would be very poor stylistically and would annoy the reader, the word 'said' does not seem to annoy the reader to anything like the same degree, or indeed at all. It's as if the reader's eye passes over the word without seeing it as an irritation when it's repeated.

I'm not saying you should never use alternatives to the standard basic speech indicator words, but I need to warn you that for me as a literary agent and a publisher, one of the sure signs of an unprofessional novel is when I notice that the writer is getting themselves into a terrible tangle with trying to think of complex speech indicator words when they could simply use the basic ones. I've seen words such as 'interceded,' 'postulated,' 'extemporised,' 'countered,' although maybe 'countered' is occasionally not too bad. The worst one I've ever seen is 'ejaculated' which does in fact mean to speak loudly as well as the other, more familiar meaning.

No, be willing to stick with 'said' and the other familiar speech indicator words except that occasionally you might like to venture into 'interrupted,' 'averred,' 'emphasised.' I'm not laying down a hard and fast rule that you should never use more complex speech indicator words but if you do want to use them keep them to the minimum because after all the point of the speech indicator is not to draw attention to the fact you possess a thesaurus but rather to make sure your reader knows which of your characters in saying your sparkling dialogue.

It's very common, by the way, for novelists to confine their scenes to scenes where there are only two characters, if you think about your own social life,

I think it's a fair bet that in any given week when you're being socially active, you probably have social situations where there's more than you and one other person. If there are three or more people in the scene, you absolutely *must* make clear to the reader who is saying what. This unfortunately means that just because you've had a couple of characters talking to each other quite a lot to the exclusion of other characters in the scene, you can't assume that the reader will simply accept that when another line of dialogue comes it's from the person who didn't just recently speak. No, you need to indicate who says what. But here's a nice technique for you which will help you a great deal. This technique is to remember the following simple and extremely important rule:

If you give an action to the character who is speaking and then put the dialogue in the next sentence without starting a new paragraph, the reader will assume that the person who did the action is the person who is speaking.

For example:

Ruth stared at John. 'Marry you? Are you delusional?'

Notice that there's no need to use a speech indicator here because it's absolutely clear to the reader that Ruth is the one saying the line of dialogue. By the way, if you *don't* want the person who did the action to be recognised as the speaker, then simply start the line of dialogue on a new paragraph. For example:

Ruth stared at John.

'I know I wouldn't be much of a husband, but I do love you.'

'Marry you? Are you delusional?'

We see there that it is clear that John is speaking the first line of dialogue even though that's made obvious by the fact that he refers to himself as being her potential husband. The point is that the usual formatting in any work of fiction necessitates the use of a new paragraph when the speaker changes.

Following this rule will also make it easier for your reader to work out who is saying what although you will still often need to put speech indicators in.

There are exceptions: sometimes you might want to write a long paragraph in which the speakers change without you creating a new paragraph; that might occur for example when you want to give a summary of a conversation in a fairly 'tell' kind of way without making it 'show' but that's technique's fairly advanced and for the time being I would simply suggest that you follow the rules I have proposed above.

Appendix 2:

Poetry corner

Here are two poems for you. Poetry is a kind of fiction writing, although in many ways it's easier to write a poem than a novel because whereas a novel has to exist in a social framework it needs to be depicted relatively realistically - even fantasy books need to be realistic in their presentation of events and locations, the novel seems to work best when being fairly realistic generally. On the other hand, poems can be, to use a wonderful phrase of the late poet Philip Larkin, 'a single emotional spearpoint'. I haven't included a section on poetry in this book as it's about prose fiction, but writing poems can sometimes help you understand the basis for a novel you might want to write; for example, you could write a poem about the main character in that novel and see if he or she becomes interesting enough in the poem for you to want to write a whole novel about him or her.

I used to write poetry quite often when I was younger at university - any man who went to Oxford University in the 1970s and who had about as much chance of finding a girlfriend as a golfer does in hitting a ball to the moon was likely to write poetry quite often. This poem I wrote more recently while staying with a good friend in Romney Marsh one November night. Romney Marsh is not as damp as the name suggests, it is nowadays a drained marsh. Still the area - which is located in south-east Kent, near the sea, is wonderfully romantic and full of legends and myths. One November night in 2015, after my friend Briony had gone to sleep and I was sitting late at night in the conservatory of her home, I thought of a visit I'd made not long before to New Romney church where I'd seen a rather pathetic gravestone of a young German sailor who died while visiting Kent and this poem seemed to me to evoke what I felt, not about that unfortunate sailor, but about Romney Marsh generally, on that windy November night.

The German sailor

Outside, beyond the double glazing
Of this house on Romney Marsh -
This comfy, wealthy home with
Warm rooms, settees and armchairs
And a larder full of food - tonight,
Past midnight, I sit here alone and hear
The rain and wind cry all around me,
Screeching endlessly out to sea
And marshwards, across the dykes
And jet-black fields of melancholy sheep.

And I remember, a year or so ago
Walking, alone, in the graveyard
Of the old, old church here in New Romney

One winter afternoon, and seeing
The tombstone of a young German sailor -
I think he was seventeen or so -
Who died while in harbour here
About a century ago. I don't know how;
Maybe a foolish punch in a tavern
Did more harm than the puncher meant,
Or perhaps some fever, caught at sea,
Shrivelled his life into a coffined husk.

I think of him now, while I'm safe here and warm
I think of him lying alone and cold -
His neighbours skulls and jigsaws of bones -
Out in the darkness and the wind,
Far from home forever,
Here, in a salty part of this foreign marsh;
Where tonight, to my surprise,
I feel at home.

The other poem is by my friend The Conrad Press writer Bridget Nolan, and is the titular poem of her poetry collection *A Walk with Charles Dickens & other poems* which The Conrad Press published in 2018. This poem seems singularly appropriate to include in view of Dickens often being mentioned here in *Writing Fiction*.

I love this poem for its wonderful atmosphere, the unpredictability of the rhymes and scansion, and the lovely sense it gives us that a writer's magic and mystique can completely triumph over death.

A Walk with Charles Dickens

I took a walk with Charles Dickens last night,
It was dark and my chest felt quite tight.
'Don't worry,' he said, 'old Marley is dead,
There's nothing to give you a fright.'

I couldn't shake off my dread sense of fear,
Magwitch, I felt sure, was skulking quite near.
'That convict,' he said, 'is certainly dead,
For he's been quiet and gone this whole year.'

From the High Street we turned into Crow Lane,
We reached Satis House and Charles lifted his cane.
'That, my dear,' he said, 'is where she lay dead,
After years of poison and pain.'

Just then, in The Vines, I thought I saw Pip
With his arm held loosely on Estella's hip.
CD saw them too and I watched,
As a quiver danced on his lip.

At the castle I asked him about Edwin Drood.
'My dear,' he sighed, 'I'm not really in the mood
To reflect on his fate.'
And I knew to persist would seem rude.

We strolled slowly to the Bull Inn,
Where quite a commotion was heard from within.
'I do hope Pickwick is not in some scrape,'
Mr Dickens said with a sly grin.

We paused outside old Guildhall Court,
Where Dickens seemed lost in deep thought.
'In there,' he whispered, 'fates are decided
And many hard lessons are taught.'

At Eastgate House we boarded a carriage,
Traversed the High Street and went over the bridge
To Cooling marshes, where the fog grew thick.
It was here where young Pip showed such courage.

Dickens led me to the chalet at Gad's Hill Place
And I'll never forget the look on his jocular face;
All those people his famed works presented,
Play their part in our great human race.

I glimpsed his literary genius,
Included today on every syllabus.
I felt the energy in that chalet,
My privilege was wondrous.

I took a walk with Charles Dickens last night,
We wandered around as the dark turned to light.
'I must go now,' he smiled, kissed my trembling hand,
And with that he vanished from sight.

Appendix 3:

A short story I wrote in the spring of 2011 in the aftermath of a break-up with a lady I had loved very much. I've changed her name and her sister's name but kept her father's name as it really was.

Alice and the baguettes

That August morning, Ed and I decided to try to reclaim the pond for the carp, assuming they still existed.

The pond was in the park surrounding the family's French country house, the Villa of Sequoias, and was about the length and breadth of an average-sized suburban lawn, though infinitely more mysterious.

The water's surface was almost covered with tiny suffocating platelets of green duckweed, except in many places where a riot of darker green water-lilies, some insolently thrusting star-shaped white flowers a foot into the air, completed an even more merciless stranglehold.

Alice told me that the pond had once been full of carp. She said that her father, Ed, who'd retired about a decade ago, had enjoyed many a pleasant summer afternoon fishing for them.

I was an angler too, though only a casual one, yet what

Alice said about the carp captured my imagination at once. Every angler, even an occasional one like me, has a cherished fantasy of discovering a secret pond or lake somewhere full of great, half-mystical, pot-bellied carp or tench which, never fished for, don't fear a baited hook.

But there were no carp visible now in this choked stretch of stagnant water. There was just a sullen hazy silence, occasionally punctuated by the soft plop of a frog as it hopped from one glossy, dark green, oval-shaped lily leaf to another.

Ed and I gazed at the stretch of weed-choked water with dismay.

'The pond's been choked up before but never like this,' Ed said, sadly, shaking his head. I knew it had been almost two months since he was last at the house.

'The carp must be staying well down,' he added, 'if we don't clear it, they'll die, even if they aren't dead already.'

I asked him how deep the pond was.

He glanced at me. 'Maybe twelve feet in the middle.'

'Then they could be pretty big,' I said. 'I wonder if they're still alive?'

I was an angler myself, so I knew something about carp: that they can survive in ponds with low oxygen levels, though in those conditions they become inactive. I was sure that if any carp were in a pond as choked as this one was, they'd be living on borrowed time.

Ed and I both agreed on that. So we were full of resolve as, right away, trying to find suitable pond-clearing tools, we started exploring the several large outbuildings of the house. Ed soon spotted a length of old rope, maybe eight or nine metres long. The question was: what could we attach to it?

The answer was a discarded rusty iron sink - evidently designed for a small room, for the sink was barely eighteen inches wide. I found it in a murky corner of one of the outbuildings.

Ed had no idea where it came from. 'It must have been there since long before we bought the house,' he said. The sink, complete with taps, seemed precisely the kind of jagged, irregularly-shaped device that could be hurled out at the end of the rope and retrieved bearing (I hoped) a harvest of duckweed, water-lily leaves, humiliated star-shaped flowers and looping tendrils of roots and stems.

In his working life, Ed had been a commercial artist, and an art director for some of London's leading advertising agencies. Nowadays, one of his favourite retirement pastimes, as well as fishing, was producing imitations of old masters so authentic they could have been sold at Sotheby's. Or at least they could if Ed hadn't, with scrupulous honesty, signed his works using his own name instead of 'Vincent', or the names of any of the other great artists whose efforts furnished Ed with an original to copy and - in many cases it seemed to me - even to improve upon.

The walls inside the house were adorned with Ed's paintings. The family - modest, loveable, unpretentious - never called their house a château, though it certainly looked like one to me.

As for Ed's paintings, they so uncannily resembled the

originals that during my week at the house I frequently found myself doing a double-take as I climbed the stairs or explored the long, winding corridors.

I mention the paintings because I discovered that August morning that Ed didn't confine his inventive ingenuity to his art. At first, after I'd tied the sink to the end of the rope, swung it a few times to build up momentum, hurled it out as far as I could into the pond, let it descend what I judged was a couple of feet below the surface, then tugged it back, the results were a disappointment. The harvest was nothing more than a few broken stems and crushed flowers.

Then Ed suggested tying to the sink the multi-spiked business end of an old wooden-handled garden rake, specially beheaded for the purpose.

His idea worked brilliantly. This time the choking lilies were no match for the strange sink/rake hybrid, and now a wonderfully satisfying mess of leaves, smashed flowers and vast amounts of root stock came back with it. I unpicked all the debris and Ed and I loaded it all onto a wheelbarrow. Once the barrow was full, Ed wheeled it away and dumped the contents in a hollow by the base of one of the nearby tall sequoia trees in the park.

I was under strict instructions from Alice not to allow him to indulge in any strenuous activity, so despite Ed's frequent pleas to chuck the sink/rake contraption out himself, I suggested it might be best if we kept to our pre-arranged job demarcation. Of course I said this gently. It was, after all, his house, and his pond.

The Villa of Sequoias is a large, square-shaped house

- four storeys high if you include its extensive dark basement with its numerous mysterious rooms that are largely unused apart from the one that contains the heating system and another accommodating the laundry machines. The external brickwork, which alternates russet and cream-coloured bricks, gives the house a jaunty look, and the sharply-roofed skylights add to this effect.

The house is just outside Noyant d'Allier, a village in the quiet, lovely, pastel-coloured agricultural region of central France called the Bourbonnais.

The river that flows close by Noyant is the Allier, and was known to the Romans at the time of their occupation of Gaul as the *Elaver*. The Romans found the river's long, broad, sluggish stream vital for transportation.

Today, a hundred generations later, the Allier is just as sluggish, broad and meandering. Largely abandoned as a means of transport, it infuses the Bourbonnais with indolent memories of the past and creates a wealth of opportunities for riverside restaurants and delightful walks.

I'd never set eyes on such a place as the Villa of Sequoias in my life, at least not from inside the gates. To be spending a week there, not having won a lottery jackpot beforehand, seemed like a dream, though without a dream's nonsensical stream of *non sequiturs*, and still less without the horrible finale when you wake up in the morning and realise that a dream was, heartbreakingly, all it was.

That I could visit the family's French mansion at all

stemmed from an extremely lucky accident: not the winning of a lottery jackpot, but something even better.

I'd met Alice the previous winter at a party in the surreally lovely Kentish town of Tenterden, in the heart of the Kentish Weald. I'd always regarded Tenterden as more like a 1950s film set than anything real. I only knew the town at all because you have to drive through it on the way from my home town of Canterbury to the Sussex seaside resort of Hastings, where I often went for the sea air in the summer and the chess in the winter.

Alice was a teacher of French in a school for kids aged from eleven to eighteen. She had a gift for inspiring her pupils. Under her tutelage many kids, who started off thinking of their French lessons as an uncool nuisance, wound up loving the language and the country.

Alice was passionate about animals, her family and friends, music, movies, cooking, dancing, travel and France. She loved wearing purple. Her clothes sense was divine. She had long, rather unruly, blond hair. She was full of life, beautiful, easy-going, thoughtful and kind, and she was socially at ease in any situation, which I knew wasn't true of me at all.

I was a professional writer, and for the past four years I'd been working harder than I'd ever worked at anything to try to learn how to write fiction. That goal had been my practically only dream.

Finally, about a month before I met Alice, I'd at last sold a novel. Yet in truth my spirit was marooned, and I was lonely despite the friends I had. I no longer wanted to immerse myself in the free life of the artist, but wished to be human again. And when I met Alice, I was sure I'd found someone I could be human again with.

For a few months, months I shall never forget, we were passionate friends. Then, inexplicably it seemed to me, her feelings began to change.

Yet we knew each other so well, and we cared about each other, and we'd always said we'd keep on being friends whatever happened, and so when she broke up with me, we did stay friends.

By the time Alice invited me to stay with her and Ed, and her younger sister Harriet, at the family's French house, Alice's love for me was gone, though not yet mine for her. She knew, I think, how hard I'd been working on my writing, and that I'd gone back to working even harder at it after things ended between us.

We made our rendezvous at the Eurotunnel terminal on a chilly August morning. I hadn't seen Alice for a month. It felt good to be with her again, and to be sitting next to her in the cosiness of the car. I would be staying at the family's house for a week. I could see Alice every day.

We reached Calais, then travelled on further south, into the heart of that dream of all writers: the sun-blessed southern lands with their olives, vines and the promise of long warm afternoons for creating art and for having conversations with friends of one's soul.

Yes, we were heading south, and far away from *la fatigue*

du Nord, an expression whose provenance I don't know but which seems admirably to sum up so much about England that often inspires a yearning to escape, including the disappointing weather; the endless obsession with money; the English tendency to over-verbalise pessimism; and, too often, the elevation of crassness and selfishness to a sort of new religion.

These are all things one wants to flee from when one feels less inclined to remember all the great qualities of England: such as the creativity and energy of the people; the splendour of the countryside; the beauty and wonder of the old towns, and the way things, generally, work pretty well considering what the alternatives could be.

So southwards we went, and ahead of us the bright yellow haze of the southern sun to which we were heading beckoned us along the neat, well-ordered and relatively empty French roads. It took us six hours to get from Calais to Noyant. As we drove, the car's air-conditioning made us oblivious to the increasing heat outside, so that when we finally pulled up near our destination, to admire the view of the Allier by a riverbank restaurant in Villeneuve-sur-Allier, the heat hit us like the remote blast of an H-bomb.

Ed and Harriet were already at the house when we arrived.

On my very first morning there, a Sunday, and the day before Ed and I conducted our maudlin inspection of the pond, I went out into Noyant before breakfast and walked to the *boulangerie*. The silent village reminded me of the setting for the film *Chocolat*. I headed round the church whose front doors had been trustingly left wide open. I passed by the small, closed *Petit Casino* grocery shop, went beyond the abandoned mine workings and then headed past a surprising park of pagodas installed as a cure for homesickness by Vietnamese families twenty years earlier who'd found a refuge here in Noyant; as in a sense I had, too.

No longer chained to my desk, I felt freer than an albatross, a man of the world, who could flit between England and France as any free-born spirit might, with little to worry about except exactly why Alice had finished with me - something I thought about very often - and how many baguettes I should buy for the loveable, unpretentious English family who had been so kind as to invite me to their French house and the park that surrounded it.

During the long August day that Ed and I spent clearing the pond, I was seized with a strange passion to make the pond so well again that nothing, *nothing* would stop the carp from having a chance of life.

I worked like a man pursuing something - some dream, some love, or perhaps some dream of love - even until the late afternoon sun began to fade and darkness started to fall. I knew I would only be happy with the results when there wasn't a single lily left in the pond.

Earlier, when it was still light, Alice sometimes came and watched us for a while. I remember one particular time, when Ed had disappeared with his laden wheelbarrow and I was again busy clearing the pond. Alice was watching me, with what seemed to me careful attention, from some distance away, close enough for me to see her face, but too far for me to tell whether her expression was a half-smile or a half-frown.

So I didn't know whether she really approved of my gusto in helping Ed clear the pond or thought I was being excessive, a vice of which she'd sometimes accused me during our passionate months.

Finally, when it was almost dark, Ed and I completely finished clearing the pond of lilies. The duckweed was reduced, too, as loads of it had come in with the harvest of lily-plants. Now, most of the pond consisted of patches of clear bright water.

After our pond-cleaning labours, I breakfasted with Ed, Alice and Harriet every morning that week, on a terrace overlooked by the largest sequoia of all, a 200-year-old eighty-foot tree that seemed to me a strange kind of mystical sentinel, watching over the family. Every day after breakfast, I went to inspect the pond and see if I could spot any carp. But so far I had seen nothing.

Alice and I were leaving the Villa of Sequoias at lunchtime on Sunday. We had had a good week together, though only as friends. I knew now what I had, in truth, known for a month but hadn't really allowed myself to accept: that the relationship was finished for ever.

That last morning, when I went to see the pond, I'd

given up any hope of seeing any life there besides the usual morose frogs. By now I was sure that the efforts Ed and I had devoted to the pond had been unrequited.

But at that moment, as I watched in amazement, I saw two dark brown dorsal fins, moving along in parallel next to each other, breaking the surface tension of the water under the weeping willow on the far side of the pond. My heart thumped and and my mouth was dry.

Each of the two dorsal fins was about a foot long.

I caught my breath. A carp's dorsal fin is about the third of the length of its body, so the two carp that were staying just below the surface must have been monsters.

I turned round to call to the family that I'd seen two carp. But I didn't, because Alice was only a few feet behind me. I'd been so absorbed, I hadn't heard her padding softly up toward me.

She was smiling.

'*I can't believe it,*' she said.

'You saw them? You saw them just now?'

Alice nodded breathlessly. 'Yes.'

She came to stand next to me. We watched the pond. For a while nothing else happened. Then, on the far right-hand side, an even larger dorsal fin broke the water, and this time for a few moments we saw not only the fin but the great wide head of a carp, a fish that must have weighed close to fifteen pounds.

With a mighty splash, the huge fish once more plunged deep.

The pond was alive again.

I glanced at Alice.

'Why wasn't I enough for you?' I murmured.

She said nothing for some moments, then her eyes met mine.

'You're too attached to your writing,' she said, softly. 'I don't mean you shouldn't be, of course you should be; I just mean it's not helpful when you think other things don't really matter, such as that how you are in company doesn't matter. How you are in company does matter to me.'

She paused for a moment then went on: 'there were often times I felt uncomfortable with you... like when we visited your friends the Richardsons and you ate all the pistachios from the glass dish! Or when you put your foot on the coffee-table that time when we were having tea with my aunt and uncle! But those were just two times... there were others as well. I loved your enthusiasm, but not your excessiveness.'

She fell silent.

I thought, briefly, of trying to defend myself. The Richardsons were always ultra-hospitable and I knew they'd have been glad I'd liked the pistachios. As for the time I'd put my foot onto the coffee table, it had just been for a minute or so, and I'd only been wearing my socks.

But I said nothing. I respected Alice, and I was her friend, and so what mattered to her mattered to me. And besides, it was too late now anyway.

'And it's not as if that's only something in the past,' Alice added, suddenly. 'You bought ten baguettes a week ago. Ten baguettes, when there are only four of us! I wasn't going to say anything about this. Ten baguettes, though! You're so excessive!'

'But... Harriet said the spare ones can go in the freezer.'

'She was just being polite. They didn't all fit. I've put the ones that didn't into the fridge, but I expect they'll be stale by now.'

Alice looked at me reproachfully, yet also I think with some affection. What I do know is that she looked very beautiful indeed; with the kind of beauty one only sees in a woman one has loved and whom one has lost forever.

Then she murmured: 'You live your life like a... well, like a hand that's always bunched up into a fist. I don't mean you're aggressive of course, I just mean you're so intense. I can't live the way you do. I'm more easy-going than you. And I work hard too; quiet times are very important to me. Now we're just friends, the differences between us don't matter so much. But please...' and for a moment I thought she might be about to cry, though she didn't. Instead, in a whisper, she added, 'let's always be friends.'

'We will. I know we will.'

I knew I didn't need to ask Alice now whether she'd been half-smiling or half-frowning when she'd watched me clearing the pond that time earlier in the week. I knew which one it had been. I also knew that it would have been futile for me to have pointed out that, perhaps, if I'd been doing the job only enthusiastically, rather than excessively, the pond wouldn't have been cleared properly, the oxygen levels would have stayed right down and the carp really might all have perished.

Would it have been worth my while mentioning this, or even that maybe some things *do* need to be done excessively if they're to be done properly? Things like writing a novel that has a chance of doing any justice to your dreams of what it could be, or fighting for a cause you believe in, or caring for what is good, and beautiful, and precious, as Alice was to me. Like I said, I respected Alice, and I

was her friend, and so what mattered to her mattered to me. And besides, it was too late now anyway.

This all happened some time ago. Alice is married now to a charming man. But she and I are still good friends, and I never feel anything less than very lucky to have met her.

I'm still looking for love, and I hope I'll find it. That's my new dream. And if I do find love again, I won't be too attached to my writing. I'll also try - I really will try my best - to be enthusiastic rather than excessive.

And Ed? Well, I think he's a very lucky man. He's got a super wife, two beautiful and fascinating daughters, and a house in France with five Van Goghs, three Rembrandts, two Gaugins, a Vermeer and several Monets and Manets on the walls.

Oh... and he has a pond with carp in it. And that summer morning, just before Alice and I left Noyant, Ed, Alice, Harriet and I spent twenty minutes feeding pieces of the stale baguettes to the carp.

Obviously hungry after their protracted indolence, they surfaced majestically in great splashless swirls to swallow the pieces of bread.

What I noticed most of all, though, were their long leathery dorsal fins.

Somehow, I couldn't help feeling that their fins were like the sails of mystical ferry-boats, conveying to the Underworld the souls of the dead.

THE END

Acknowledgements

I am very grateful to the novelist and screenwriter William Osborne, whose many credits include co-writing the wonderful movie *Twins*; to the screenwriter and movie producer Bob Gale whose three *Back to the Future* films are and will remain three of the greatest movies ever written and made; to Russell Galen (who did not agent this book but who, as I explain in it, essentially taught me how to write fiction); and to Jo Bavington-Jones for her careful proof-reading, any errors that remain are my fault, not hers.

I'm also grateful to Briony Kapoor and Irina Cusworth; to Annelisa Christensen for her inspiration; to Charlotte Mouncey for designing the book's jacket, for editorial help and for typesetting the book; to Nic Nicholas for the index; to Rory O'Grady for introducing me to the great Kipling quotation; and to the writers of The Conrad Press for being such a great community with which to work.

My much loved brother Rupert (May 2 1961 - Jan 22 2019) died tragically while I was working on this book. One of the many horrible things about missing Rupert is that I can no longer share aspects of my work with him that I would have shared in the past. For example Rupert was a great fan of the *Back to the Future* films and would have loved to know that Bob Gale helped me with this book. I plan to write a biography of Rupert, *A Scientist of Where,* later this year.

James Essinger May 2019

Index

G

H